Frommer's

W9-CEH-474

Portland
day BY day ®

2nd Edition

by Donald Olson

FrommerMedia LLC

Contents

Published by:

Frommer Media LLC

ISBN: 978-1-628-87300-9 (paper); ISBN 978-1-628-87241-5 (ebk)

Editorial Director: Pauline Frommer
Editor: Holly Hughes
Production Editor: Erin Geile
Photo Editor: Helen Stallion
Cartographer: Liz Puhl
Compositor: Julie Trippetti
Indexer: Maro RioFrancos

Front cover photos, left to right: Mount Hood, © tusharkoley / Shutterstock.com. Lion at Oregon Zoo, with kind permission: Oregon Zoo. Iconic sign in downtown Portland, © Jess Kraft / Shutterstock.com.

Back cover photo: Columbia River Gorge, © Anton Foltin / Shutterstock.com

For information on our other products and services, please go to Frommers.com.

Frommer's also publishes its books in a variety of electronic formats. Some content that appears in print may not be available in electronic formats.

Manufactured in China

5   4   3   2   1

About this Guide

Organizing your time. That's what this guide is all about.

Other guides give you long lists of things to see and do and then expect you to fit the pieces together. The Day by Day guides are different. These guides tell you the best of everything, and then they show you how to see it in the smartest, most time-efficient way. Our authors have designed detailed itineraries organized by time, neighborhood, or special interest. And each tour comes with a bulleted map that takes you from stop to stop.

Planning a first-time trip to Portland with the kids? Looking for great ways to explore the Rose City by bike? Or maybe you want to know how to get the most out of the city even on a rainy Pacific Northwestern day. Whatever your interest or schedule, the Day by Days give you the smartest routes to follow. Not only do we take you to the top attractions, hotels, and restaurants, but we also help you access those special moments that locals get to experience—those "finds" that turn tourists into travelers.

The Day by Days are also your top choice if you're looking for one complete guide for all your travel needs. The best hotels and restaurants for every budget, the greatest shopping values, the wildest nightlife—it's all here.

Why should you trust our judgment? Because our authors personally visit each place they write about. They're an independent lot who say what they think and would never include places they wouldn't recommend to their best friends. They're also open to suggestions from readers. If you'd like to contact them, please send your comments our way at Support@FrommerMedia.com, and we'll pass them on.

Enjoy your Day by Day guide—the most helpful travel companion you can buy. And have the trip of a lifetime.

About the Author

Donald Olson is a travel writer, novelist, and playwright. His travel stories have appeared in *The New York Times, National Geographic,* and other national publications. His travel guides for Frommer's include *Seattle Day by Day; Seattle, Portland & the Oregon Coast;* and *Berlin Day by Day.* His book *The Pacific Northwest Garden Tour* was named by *Library Journal* as one of the best reference books of 2014. His new book, *The California Garden Tour,* will be published by Timber Press in 2017.

An Additional Note

Please be advised that travel information is subject to change at any time—and this is especially true of prices. We therefore suggest that you write or call ahead for confirmation when making your travel plans. The authors, editors, and publisher cannot be held responsible for the experiences of readers while traveling. Your safety is important to us, however, so we encourage you to stay alert and be aware of your surroundings.

Star Ratings, Icons & Abbreviations

Every hotel, restaurant, and attraction listing in this guide has been ranked for quality, value, service, amenities, and special features using a **star-rating system.** Hotels, restaurants, attractions, shopping, and nightlife are rated on a scale of zero stars (recommended) to three stars (exceptional). In addition to the star-rating system, we also use a **kids** **icon** to point out the best bets for families. Within each tour, we recommend cafes, bars, or restaurants where you can take a break. Each of these stops appears in a shaded box marked with a coffee-cup-shaped bullet ☕.

The following **abbreviations** are used for credit cards:

AE	American Express	DISC	Discover	V	Visa
DC	Diners Club	MC	MasterCard		

Travel Resources at Frommers.com

Frommer's travel resources don't end with this guide. Frommer's website, **www.frommers.com**, has travel information on more than 4,000 destinations. We update features regularly, giving you instant access to the most current trip-planning information available, and the best airfares, lodging rates, and car rental bargains. You can listen to podcasts, connect with other Frommers.com members through our active-reader forums, share your travel photos, read blogs from guidebook editors and fellow travelers, and much more.

A Note on Prices

In the "Take a Break" (coffee-cup icon) and "Best Bets" sections of this book, we have used a system of dollar signs to show a range of costs for 1 night in a hotel (the price of a double-occupancy room) or the cost of an entree at a restaurant. Use the following table to decipher the dollar signs:

Cost	Hotels	Restaurants
$	under $125	under $15
$$	$125–$225	$15–$20
$$$	$225–$325	$20–$30
$$$$	$325–$400	$30–$40
$$$$$	over $400	over $40

How to Contact Us

In researching this book, we discovered many wonderful places—hotels, restaurants, shops, and more. We're sure you'll find others. Please tell us about them, so we can share the information with your fellow travelers in upcoming editions. If you were disappointed with a recommendation, we'd love to know that, too. Please write to: Support@FrommerMedia.com

16 Favorite
Moments

16 Favorite Moments

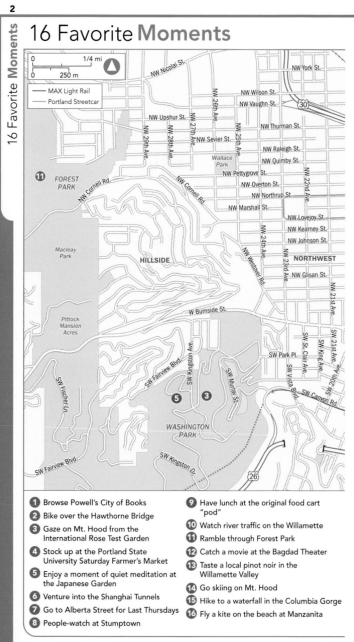

0 | 1/4 mi
0 | 250 m

— MAX Light Rail
— Portland Streetcar

NW Nicolai St.
NW York St.
NW Wilson St.
NW Vaughn St.
30
NW Upshur St.
NW Thurman St.
NW Sevier St.
NW Raleigh St.
Wallace Park
NW Quimby St.
NW Pettygrove St.
FOREST PARK
NW Cornell Rd.
NW Overton St.
NW Cornell Rd.
NW Northrup St.
NW Marshall St.
NW Lovejoy St.
NW Kearney St.
NW Johnson St.
Macleay Park
NORTHWEST
HILLSIDE
NW Glisan St.
Pittock Mansion Acres
W Burnside St.
SW Park Pl.
SW St. Clair Ave.
SW Fairview Blvd.
SW Kingston Ave.
SW Murray St.
SW Vista Blvd.
SW Canyon Rd.
SW Fischer Ln.
5
3
WASHINGTON PARK
SW Kingston Dr.
SW Fairview Blvd.
26

1 Browse Powell's City of Books
2 Bike over the Hawthorne Bridge
3 Gaze on Mt. Hood from the International Rose Test Garden
4 Stock up at the Portland State University Saturday Farmer's Market
5 Enjoy a moment of quiet meditation at the Japanese Garden
6 Venture into the Shanghai Tunnels
7 Go to Alberta Street for Last Thursdays
8 People-watch at Stumptown
9 Have lunch at the original food cart "pod"
10 Watch river traffic on the Willamette
11 Ramble through Forest Park
12 Catch a movie at the Bagdad Theater
13 Taste a local pinot noir in the Willamette Valley
14 Go skiing on Mt. Hood
15 Hike to a waterfall in the Columbia Gorge
16 Fly a kite on the beach at Manzanita

Previous page: Downtime on Cannon Beach.

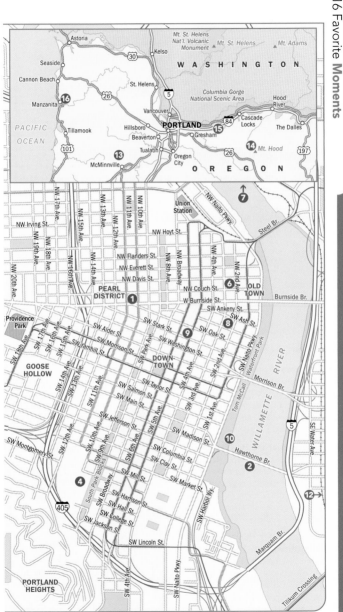

Sometimes Portland seems almost too good to be true. Just try to get locals to stop rhapsodizing about the cuisine, the live-ability and bike-ability, the great neighborhoods, the nearby mountains and ocean, the beer and wine and coffee and—see what I mean? Once a gritty younger sibling to Seattle, the City of Roses has roared into its own in recent years, becoming a nationwide magnet for creative, outdoorsy folks young, old, and in-between—anyone who wants a vibrant, forward-thinking city that's also manageable. Now Portland swings far above its weight class in everything from coffee roasting to sustainability. Here are just a few of the highlights.

Cycling across the Hawthorne Bridge.

1 **Browse Powell's City of Books.** The world's top independent bookstore fills an entire city block (and that's just this branch) with over 1.5 million new and used books. It's pure bibliophile nirvana. See p 77.

2 **Bike over the Hawthorne Bridge.** Bikes are a way of life in Portland, and there's no better way to join the rolling masses than to take a spin across the Hawthorne Bridge over the Willamette River, especially in the evening. See p 93.

3 **Gaze on Mt. Hood from the International Rose Test Garden.** The flowers are gorgeous and the views are even better up here in Washington Park. On a clear day you can see multiple snowcapped volcanoes on the eastern horizon, with Mt. Hood at center stage. See p 13.

4 **Stock up at the Portland State University Saturday Farmer's Market.** Local organic produce, baked goods, food carts, and family-friendly entertainment make the Saturday-morning market at PSU a weekend must-do from March through December. See p 82.

5 **Enjoy a moment of quiet meditation at the Portland Japanese Garden.** The most authentic of its kind outside of Japan, the Portland Japanese Garden offers countless serene nooks for contemplating the meticulously manicured rocks and greenery—or your own navel. See p 15.

The International Rose Test Garden.

A pond reflection at the Portland Japanese Garden.

6 Venture into the Shanghai Tunnels. Take a guided underground tour for a peek into Portland's sordid past, when drunken sailors and drifters were "Shanghaied"—kidnapped and forced to work on oceangoing ships. See p 34.

7 Go to Alberta Street for Last Thursdays. In the rest of the city, it's the first Thursday of every month that brings the gallery openings. Up on Alberta, though, they go with the "Keep Portland Weird" theme and turn the whole street into one big party of art, music, and eccentricity on the *last* Thursday. See p 59.

8 People-watch at Stumptown. The quintessential Portland coffee roaster runs a handful of coffee shops that double as primo spots for eyeballing and tattoo-spotting. The downtown branch has the best field of view. See p 62.

9 Have lunch at the original food cart "pod." On SW 5th Avenue between Oak and Stark streets, the line-up of food carts offers you a choice from a global variety of dishes including Cuban, Thai, Indian, pizza, or "Bulkogi Fusion" (that is, Korean tacos), to name just a few. See p 69.

Vintage flicks at the Bagdad Theater.

Skiing on Mt. Hood.

⑩ Watch river traffic on the Willamette. The Eastbank Esplanade's floating walkway is a great place to spot barges, sailboats, dragon boats, and other water craft. Plus it offers a primo view of the downtown skyline at sunset. See p 67.

⑪ Ramble through Forest Park. Eight square miles of wild forest, streams, gorges, and fern-covered hillsides wait on the west side of the city, with more than 70 miles of hiking trails and fire roads to explore. See p 86.

⑫ Catch a movie at the Bagdad Theater. Order a microbrew and a slice of pizza and enjoy a second-run movie in this fully restored 1927 movie palace in the lively Hawthorne District. Stay for dinner or a drink afterward, or venture down the block for dozens of other nightlife options. See p 127.

⑬ Taste a local pinot noir in the Willamette Valley. South of Portland, the mild climate and volcanic soil of the Willamette River Valley is ideal for growing wine grapes, which translates into more than 400 wineries. See p 148.

⑭ Go skiing on Mt. Hood, no matter what the season. It's the only place in the country with lift-accessible skiing year-round. Or just enjoy the views from the 1927 Timberline Lodge, whose snowbound exterior doubled for the hotel in *The Shining*. (The service here is much better, though.) See p 140.

⑮ Hike to a waterfall in the Columbia Gorge. There are plenty to choose from, but from the Oneonta Trailhead, one easy loop leads you to four waterfalls, including a cascade that you walk behind. See p 144.

⑯ Fly a kite on the beach at Manzanita. The ocean may be too chilly up here to enjoy without a wet suit, but Oregon's shoreline is as spectacular as any on the West Coast, and the charming beach town of Manzanita is within day-trip distance of Portland. See p 157. ●

Pony Tail Falls in the Columbia Gorge.

1 The Best Full-Day Tours

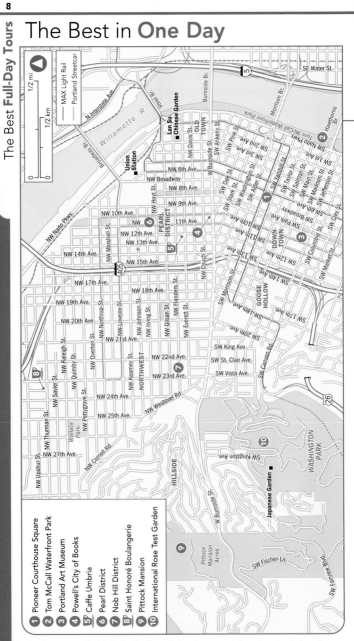

- 1 Pioneer Courthouse Square
- 2 Tom McCall Waterfront Park
- 3 Portland Art Museum
- 4 Powell's City of Books
- 5 Caffe Umbria
- 6 Pearl District
- 7 Nob Hill District
- 8 Saint Honoré Boulangerie
- 9 Pittock Mansion
- 10 International Rose Test Garden

Previous page: The iconic Portlandia sculpture downtown is based on the city's seal.

This full-day ramble starts in downtown Portland and ventures up into the West Hills, giving a great overview—literally—of the city's top offerings. After swinging by the riverfront, you'll probably want to trade your walking shoes for a streetcar or bus to reach the final few stops. START: **MAX to Pioneer Courthouse/SW 6th Ave. or Pioneer Square South. Bus: 1, 12, 19, or 94 to Pioneer Courthouse Square.**

Governor Tom McCall Waterfront Park.

1 ★★ **Pioneer Courthouse Square.** "Portland's living room" anchors downtown and embodies the Rose City itself in all its eclectic, endearing scruffiness and charm. It's a place to people-watch and mingle, filled with shoppers, locals on lunch break, and everyone in between. You'll almost always find some kind of outdoor event going on, be it a farmer's market (Mon June–Oct), Italian food festival, rock concert, or sand castle–building competition. An information center and a TriMet ticket office are available to visitors. The graceful cupola of the Pioneer Courthouse at the east end of the square has been a Portland landmark since 1875. ⏱ 15 min. Btw. SW 6th Ave., Broadway, Yamhill & Morrison sts. ☎ 503/223-1613. www.thesquarepdx.org.

Visitor center Mon–Fri 8:30am–5:30pm, Sat 10am–4pm. MAX: Pioneer Courthouse. Bus: 1, 12, 19, or 94.

2 ★★★ kids **Governor Tom McCall Waterfront Park.** What a different place Portland would be if this 1½-mile green swath along the west bank of the Willamette River was still a freeway, as it was in the past. Now it's one of the city's best places to stroll, bike, or enjoy one of the many yearly festivals held here. In the hotter months, kids love cooling off in the Salmon Street Springs fountain at Salmon Street, with 185 computer-controlled water jets. The ever-popular Saturday Market (also held on Sundays) is held beneath the Burnside Bridge, just past the 1947 stern-wheeler that houses the Oregon

Maritime Center and Museum (see p 53). Farther down, the Japanese American Historical Plaza at Davis Street commemorates Oregon's Japanese-American citizens interned during World War II with poetry-inscribed rocks and spring-flowering cherry trees. ① *1 hr. Naito Parkway btw. Steel Bridge & RiverPlace Marina. Open daily. MAX: Yamhill District, Oak/SW 1st Ave., or Old Town/Chinatown.*

❸ ★ **Portland Art Museum.** Founded in 1892, the Northwest's oldest art museum is a one-stop overview of art from regional Native American artifacts to contemporary painting and photography. The permanent collection includes more than 5,000 objects by Northwest artists and a 100-item cache of English silver. Recent acquisitions include a Rembrandt Peale portrait of George Washington and van

One of many rooms at the vast Powell's City of Books.

Gogh's *The Ox-Cart*. It's also the home of the Northwest Film Center, which shows classic, foreign, and independent works through the year. ① *1½ hr. 1219 SW Park Ave.* ☎ *503/226-2811. www.portland artmuseum.org. Admission $20 adults, $17 seniors over 54, free for kids under 18, free for everyone 5–8pm the 4th Fri of the month. Tues, Wed, Sat & Sun 10am–5pm, Thurs–Fri 10am–8pm. Streetcar: Art Museum.*

❹ ★★★ **kids** **Powell's City of Books.** Few cities identify with a bookstore as closely as Portland does with Powell's, the world's largest—and many would say best—independent bookseller. Powell's downtown flagship store is like a metropolis of literature, filling a full square block with over 1.5 million new and used books spread through nine color-coded rooms. You'll need a map, and probably a cup of coffee from the World Cup coffee shop, but you'll be rewarded with the ultimate bibliophile browsing experience. Powell's hosts regular free author readings. Don't miss the Rare Books Room, full of signed first editions, plus a priceless 1814 account of Lewis and Clark's journey. ① *1 hr. 1005 W. Burnside Ave.* ☎ *503/228-4651. www.powells.com. Daily 9am–11pm; Rare Book Room Sat–Sun 11am–7pm. Streetcar: NW Couch. Bus: 20.*

smell·bound (smel-ˌbaÜnd) *adj* : held as if under a spell by the scent of books

For an excellent cappuccino and maybe a panini sandwich or a gelato, head over to ❺ **Caffè Umbria,** a casually sophisticated cafe/bar in the true Italian style. *303 NW 12th Ave.* ☎ *503/241-5300. www.caffeumbria.com. $.*

Hanging out by the streetcar line in the Pearl District.

6 ★★ kids **Pearl District.** Continue your tour on foot, or hop on the Portland Streetcar NS line at NW Couch Street for a leisurely trip through the heart of Portland's newest and most successful neighborhood. Over the past couple of decades, this former industrial warehouse area has been transformed by a mix of condo and rental buildings, art galleries, cafes, urban parks like **Jamison Square** (see p 49) and **Tanner Springs Park** (see p 49), small specialty stores, and restaurants galore. See p 48 for more details. ⏱ *1 hr. Bounded by W Burnside St., NW Naito Pkwy., NW 14th Ave. & Broadway. Streetcar: NS line from NW Couch to NW 23rd Ave.*

7 ★★ **Nob Hill District.** Northwest Portland's walkable commercial district centers on two streets: NW 23rd Avenue, lined with shops and boutiques, and NW 21st Avenue, with more restaurants (the Portland Streetcar NS line stops at both streets). National retailers like Urban Outfitters and Pottery Barn cluster at the south end of NW 23rd near Burnside. Head north for boutiques selling vintage clothes, locally made jewelry, wine, specialty foods, or New Age books and paraphernalia. Every block has somewhere to browse, nibble, or rest. ⏱ *1½ hr. NW 23rd Ave. btw. Burnside & Thurman sts; NW 21st Ave. btw. Burnside & Northrup sts. Streetcar: NW 23rd & Marshall. Bus: 15.*

Ticket Deal

If you plan on making the rounds of the city's major sights, save money with one of four different Portland Attractions Passes. The **Big Pass** ($55 per adult) covers the Portland Art Museum, Lan Su Chinese Garden, Oregon History Museum, Zoo, Pittock Mansion, Children's Museum, Japanese Garden, and World Forestry Center. For more modest itineraries, opt for the separate **Washington Park Pass** ($33), **Downtown Pass** ($22), or **Garden Pass** ($19). Each is valid for 5 days and available only online at www.travel portland.com.

The Pittock Mansion's elegant music room.

Sit at a sidewalk table or take a seat at the communal table indoors, both good spots to linger over a hot or cold drink and a delicious pastry. *2335 NW Thurman St. (at 23rd Ave.).* ☎ *503/445-4342. www. sainthonorebakery.com. $.*

Named after the patron saint of bakers, the cozy **8** **Saint Honoré Boulangerie** cafe and bakery serves French pastries and rustic breads fresh from the clay firebrick oven.

9 ★★ **Pittock Mansion.** The home of Portland pioneer Henry Pittock—publisher of the *Oregonian* newspaper and part of the first party to climb Mt. Hood—gazes over the city from 1,000 feet above in the West Hills, at the edge of Forest Park. Built in 1914, the 23-room French Renaissance Revival chateau combines Northwest materials and workmanship with Turkish, French, and English design touches, along with newfangled (for its time) inventions like an intercom system and an elevator. The view from the front yard, east across the city as far as Mt. Hood, is worth the trip in itself. You can hike here along the Wildwood Trail from Washington Park or Forest Park. *3229 NW Pittock Dr.* ☎ *503/823-3623. www.pittockmansion.org. Open 11am–4pm daily, 10am–5pm*

A Rose City by Any Other Name?

Portland can thank Leo Samuel, founder of Standard Insurance, for its flowery nickname. Samuel, who lived here in the late 19th century, was an enthusiastic rose gardener who would leave clippers by his bushes so that other people could help themselves to blossoms. Other gardeners followed suit, and word soon spread that the damp city on the Willamette was a hotbed for these temperamental flowers. Roses are still grown outside the Standard Insurance Company's home office on SW 6th Avenue between Salmon and Taylor streets downtown. Portland's other nickname, "Stumptown," comes from—you guessed it—the logging industry, while the popular shorthand PDX comes from the airline code for Portland International Airport.

The International Rose Test Garden.

July & Aug, closed Jan. Admission $10 adults, $9 seniors over 64, $7 kids 6–18.

🔟 ★★ **International Rose Test Garden.** Portland's nickname, "The City of Roses," reaches an apogee high in the hills of Washington Park, where about 10,000 rosebushes thrive in the oldest continuously operating official garden of its kind. Founded in 1917, the garden follows its mission to test and preserve new rose hybrids, but even the non-greenthumbed will love the combination of blooms and views. Kiddie-size blooms fill the Miniature Rose Garden, while a wall in the Shakespeare Garden, home to plants mentioned in the Bard's plays, features a fitting quote from *The Two Noble Kinsmen*: "Of all flowers methinks a rose is best." (For more Washington Park attractions, see p 88.) 🕐 *30 min. In summer, go early in the morning or in the evening for smaller crowds. 400 SW Kingston Ave.* ☎ *503/823-3636. www.rosegardenstore.org. Open daily 7:30am–9pm. Free admission. Free guided tours given June–Sept at 11:30am Tues & 1pm Sat & Sun. MAX: Washington Park Station. (In summer, a bus shuttle runs from the station to the gardens every 15 min.) Bus: 63.*

The Best in **Two Days**

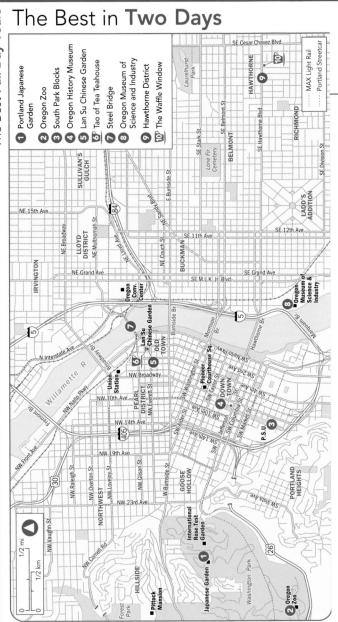

1 Portland Japanese Garden
2 Oregon Zoo
3 South Park Blocks
4 Oregon History Museum
5 Lan Su Chinese Garden
6 Tao of Tea Teahouse
7 Steel Bridge
8 Oregon Museum of Science and Industry
9 Hawthorne District
10 The Waffle Window

······· MAX Light Rail
······· Portland Streetcar

If you have 2 days, follow the preceding tour for your first day, then start the second one in Washington Park. From there you'll head downhill and across the river to OMSI, ending up in Portland's liveliest southeast district. If you time it right, you'll finish the day with another hilltop sunset, this time from the top of Mt. Tabor.
START: **Washington Park. MAX Oregon Zoo. Bus 63.**

❶ ★★★ Portland Japanese Garden. This serene masterpiece of Japanese-garden design in the heart of Washington Park offers five classic Japanese garden styles, a koi pond, an authentic teahouse, and one of the best views of the city and Mount Hood. Considered the finest example of its kind outside of Japan, the 5½-acre garden fits Portland's misty, moody climate perfectly. A walking path winds through meticulously tended landscapes that change with the seasons, from the waterfall and zigzag bridge in the lush pond garden to the carefully raked patterns in the sand and stone garden. Traditional and seasonal events and exhibits, including *ikebana* (flower-arranging) and autumn moon viewing, take place throughout the year. A new visitor center by famed Japanese architect Kengo Kuma is in the works. (For more Washington Park attractions, see p 88.) ⏱ *1 hr. 611 SW Kingston Ave.* ☎ *503/223-1321. www.japanesegarden.com. Admission $9.50 adults, $7.75 seniors 62 and over, $7.75 college students with ID, $6.75 kids 6–17. Summer noon–7pm Mon, 10am–7pm Tues–Sun; winter noon–4pm Mon, 10am–4pm Tues–Sun. Free guided tours 1 & 2:30pm daily & 10:45am Tues–Sun Apr–Oct; 1pm Sat & Sun Nov–Mar. MAX: Washington Park; free bus shuttle to garden in summer. Bus: 63 (weekdays only).*

❷ ★★ kids Oregon Zoo. Started in the 1880s by a downtown druggist who collected animals from friendly sailors, Oregon's premier zoo is now home to more than 2,000 animals, including many

The Portland Japanese Garden.

A polar bear frolics at the Oregon Zoo.

threatened and endangered species. Start with the black bears, cougars, and wolves of the Pacific Northwest; then venture into an Amazon flooded forest, eyeball a Serengeti cheetah, or come nose-to-snout with a linebacker-size orangutan. Note that the animals are most active in the early morning or late afternoon. The zoo is particularly proud of its Asian Elephant breeding program, whose ranks include local celebrity Packy and baby Sam, born in 2008. (Animal-rights activists, however, have urged the zoo to retire the elephants to a sanctuary.) Hop aboard a ⅝-scale train pulled by a real steam engine, which puffs around the zoo or on a 4-mile loop to the International Rose Test Garden and Portland Japanese Garden. From June to August, the zoo hosts open-air concerts on summer evenings with local and national acts. ⓘ *1½ hr. 4001 SW Canyon Rd.* ☎ *503/226-1561. www.oregonzoo. org. Admission $13 adults, $10 seniors over 64, $8.50 kids 3–11, $4 per person the 2nd Tues of every month, show MAX ticket for $1.50*

discount. Summer 9am–6pm; fall, spring 9am–4pm; winter 10am–4pm. MAX: Washington Park. Bus: 63 (weekdays only).

❸ ★ **South Park Blocks.** Portland's first parks, set aside in 1852, are still a peaceful respite from the hubbub of downtown. Stately oaks, elms, and maples shade 12 grassy blocks between SW Salmon and SW Jackson streets. Public art on every block ranges from the heroic (statues of Teddy Roosevelt and Lincoln) to the abstract (three granite blocks titled "Peace Chant"). The southern end, part of Portland State University, is closed to car traffic and home to the Portland Farmer's Market (see p 82) on Saturday mornings from spring through fall. ⓘ *30 min. Open daily.*

❹ ★ **Oregon History Museum.** Delve into the past of Oregon and the entire Pacific Northwest at this collection, run by the Oregon Historical Society on the South Park Blocks. The main permanent exhibit is the award-winning "Oregon My Oregon," which takes up an entire floor and includes a 9,000-year-old sagebrush sandal and the lunch counter from Newberry's, a famous downtown eatery. Other exhibits, permanent and traveling, cover topics such as Lewis and Clark, the Oregon Trail, western Native baskets, and Portland's major league soccer team, the Timbers. ⏱ *30 min. 1200 SW Park Ave.* ☎ *503/306-5198. www. ohs.org. Admission $11; students over 18 & seniors over 60 $9; children 6–18 $5. Tues–Sat 10am–5pm; Sun noon–5pm. MAX: SW 6th & Madison sts. Streetcar: Art Museum. Bus: 6, 38, 43, 45, 55, 58, 68, 92, or 96.*

⑤ ★★★ Lan Su Chinese Garden. Always a surprise amid the general shabbiness of what's left of Chinatown, this hidden gem is a fully authentic Ming Dynasty–style classical Chinese garden complete with lake, bridges, elaborate pavilions, and a two-story teahouse. All the wooden buildings, decorative windows, and 500 tons of rock were shipped in from Suzhou, China, and reassembled by a team of workers, also from Suzhou. Every season highlights the carefully planned landscape and plantings in a different way, from spring blooms and fall leaves to the bare branches of winter. ⏱ *45 min. Entrance at NW 3rd Ave. & Everett St. www.lansu garden.org. Admission $9.50 adults, $8.50 seniors 62 and over, $7 students & kids 6–18. Free tours daily at noon & 1pm. Open daily, summer 10am–6pm; winter 10am–5pm. MAX: Old Town Chinatown. Bus: 4, 8, 9, 16, 35, 44, or 77.*

What better way to recharge than over a cup of oolong at **⑥ Tao of Tea Teahouse** inside the Tower of Cosmic Reflections, gazing over Lake Zither in the Lan Su Chinese Garden? Along with a huge selection of teas, the teahouse offers a short list of sweets and nibbles. ☎ *503/224-8455. $.*

⑦ ★ Steel Bridge. Of all Portland's bridges, this 210-foot span, built in 1912, offers the most ways to cross the Willamette River. The upper deck carries cars and MAX

A mellow afternoon along the South Park Blocks.

The iconic Steel Bridge crosses the Willamette River.

light rail, while the lower accommodates trains, cyclists, and pedestrians, the latter two on a cantilevered walkway that connects Waterfront Park to the Vera Katz Eastbank Esplanade. Bridge buffs ahoy: It's the world's only double-deck vertical lift bridge whose lower deck can lift independently of the upper one. It's the second-oldest vertical lift bridge in North America. (Hawthorne Bridge—also in Portland—is the oldest.) ⏱ *15 min. Btw. NW Naito Pkwy./NW Glisan St. & N Interstate Ave./NE Multnomah St.*

⑧ ★ kids Oregon Museum of Science and Industry. Set,

fittingly, in a former power plant on the east bank of the Willamette River, OMSI celebrates knowledge and technology in all forms. Hands-on exhibits demonstrate everything from aging to nanotechnology, including a replica of the Gemini space capsule and a chemistry lab for mixing concoctions (safely). You can also catch a show in the Omnimax theater, stargaze in the largest planetarium in the Northwest, or head out to the river to tour the 210-foot USS *Blueback*, the country's last diesel submarine. Adults can avoid the near-constant crowds of schoolchildren by coming for

Travel Tip

How about a vacation from driving? Portland's extensive interconnected system of buses, streetcars, and light-rail trains (MAX) lets you do just that. It's all operated by Tri-Met—go to **www. trimet.org** for a handy set of easy-to-use navigational tools to help you plan your trip from point A to B. (For streetcar information go to **www.portlandstreetcar.org**). MAX and streetcar routes operate on an honor system; buy your tickets before you board at vending machines at every stop. Buses require a ticket, a pass, or exact change. See p 164 for more information on Portland's public transportation.

"OMSI After Dark" evening events, open only to the 21-and-over crowd. ⏰ *1 hr. 1945 SE Water Ave.* ☎ *503/797-4000. www.omsi.edu. Tues–Sun 9:30am–5:30pm. Admission $14 adults, $9.50 seniors over 62 & kids 3–13, $2 per person the 1st Sun of every month. Submarine, planetarium & Omnimax tickets are extra; various combination deals are available. Bus: 4, 6, 10, 14, 31, 32, or 33. Streetcar: OMSI.*

❾ ★ Hawthorne District. Portland's epicenter of eclecticism stretches along Hawthorne Boulevard between 30th and 42nd avenues, packed with restaurants, cafes, bars, boutiques, thrift stores, and theaters. Most of the action is concentrated between 34th and 39th avenues, including the historic Bagdad Theater & Pub (see p 127) and a branch of Powell's Books. It's an easily walkable stretch, with plenty of options for shopping and noshing. See p 63 for more details. *Bus: 14.*

If you still think waffles are just for breakfast, peek around the corner from the Bread and Ink Café for **❿ The Waffle Window**'s bright blue doorway, serving creative concoctions like the Three Bs (brie, basil, and pepper bacon). They also offer classic waffle toppings like berries, jam, and syrup. Sit outside at the picnic tables or inside on rainy days. *3610 SE Hawthorne Blvd.* ☎ *503/239-4756. www.waffle window.com. $.*

The USS Blueback *submarine outside the Oregon Museum of Science and Industry (OMSI).*

The Best in **Three Days**

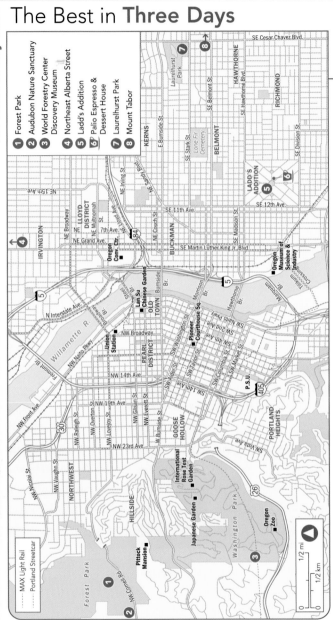

--- MAX Light Rail
····· Portland Streetcar

aving 3 days to play with lets you venture farther afield; in this case, into the offbeat, artsy northeast section of town. Plus you'll have time to explore a few of Portland's outdoor options in more depth, including one of the largest urban parks in the country. START: **Bus 15 to NW Thurman & 29th Ave. (Lower MacLeay Park).**

1 ★★ **Forest Park.** Portland's leafy backyard covers 8 square miles of the West Hills, making it the country's largest urban forest reserve. (It's over six times the size of New York's Central Park.) It's still home to many of the species that were here when explorer William Clark visited on a side trip in 1806—from bobcats and black-tailed deer to pygmy owls and woodpeckers. Small streams and over 70 miles of trails wind through the park's forested hillsides and valleys, including the popular 30-mile **Wildwood Trail,** a National Recreation Trail. (Mountain bikers are limited to access roads and fire lanes.) It's also amazingly close to downtown; the **Lower MacLeay Park** trailhead at the end of NW Upshur Street is easy to access on foot, and NW Thurman Street turns into **Leif Ericson Drive,** the park's main travel artery. From there you can

hike to the Pittock Mansion (p 91), Washington Park (p 88), or go as far as Gresham on the 40-Mile Loop from the Wildwood Trail. See p 87 for more details on Forest Park's recreation options. ⏱ *1½ hr. Numerous trail heads.* ☎ *503/823-7529. www.forestparkconservancy. org. Open daily. Dogs must be leashed. Bus: 15, 20.*

2 ★ **kids** **Audubon Nature Sanctuary.** For a quick taste of Portland's lush city-edge forests, with a close-up animal encounter or two thrown in for free, head to this 150-acre public reserve at Forest Park's southern end. Four miles of trails lead along Balch Creek and under old-growth Douglas firs, and from here you can access the Wildwood and Upper MacLeay trails in Forest Park proper. The Wildlife Care Center is Oregon's oldest and most active, giving thousands of

The Lower MacLeay Park trail head in Forest Park.

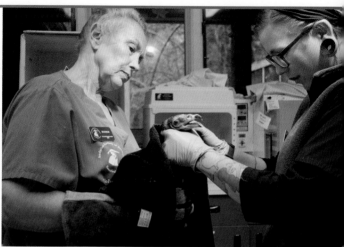

The Audubon Nature Sanctuary's Wildlife Care Center.

injured animals per year another chance at life in the wild. You never know who'll be in residence: Beavers, bald eagles, great horned owls, and turtles have all made appearances. ⏱ *1 hr. 5151 NW Cornell Rd.* ☎ *503/292-6855. www.audubonportland.org/sanctuaries. Open daily, trails dawn to dusk, care center 9am–5pm. Free admission. Bus: 15 (plus 1½-mile walk from NW 23rd & Lovejoy St.).*

❸ ★ kids **World Forestry Center Discovery Museum.** Timber is a cornerstone of Northwest history, and this small hands-on museum in Washington Park shows how important forests are to the region's past and future. Treading the sometimes-delicate line between environmental stewardship and timber extraction, it has two floors of interactive displays that range from virtual tours through the world's major types of forest to a timberjack harvester simulator. ⏱ *1 hr. 4033 SW Canyon Rd.* ☎ *503/228-1367. www.world forestry.org. Admission $5 for*

everyone ages 3 and older. 1st Wed of each month $3 per person. Open daily 10am–5pm. MAX: Washington Park. Bus: 63.

❹ ★ **Northeast Alberta Street.** From here, you have several options for how to spend the rest of your day. Looking for a case study in gentrification with a high hipster factor? Northeast Alberta Street between 15th and 33rd avenues is one of the more interesting neighborhoods on Portland's east side. The main drag is chock-full of restaurants, shops, theaters, and art galleries; see p 58 for more details. Most businesses throw their doors open on the last Thursday of every month for the city's funkiest monthly street fair, complete with music, clowns, and carefully balanced "tall bikes." ⏱ *1 hr. NE Alberta St. btw. 15th & 33rd aves.*

❺ ★ **Ladd's Addition.** Or perhaps you'd prefer this designated historic district, great for a shady walk under magnificent old elm trees that line the streets. Created by and named for William Ladd, a

19th-century mayor who had a farm here, Ladd's Addition—one of Portland's oldest planned residential districts—breaks up the east side's neat road grid into an 8-by-10-block division of diagonals and roundabouts unlike any other neighborhood on the West Coast. The neighborhood's odd road alignments leave room for four diamond-shaped gardens, each overflowing in season with roses (of course), as well as a larger circular park inside the central roundabout. ⏱ *45 min. Btw. SE Hawthorne St., Division St, 12th Ave. & 20th Ave. Bus: 4, 10, 14, or 70.*

Rest your feet and enjoy a Mexican Mocha or a slice of key lime pie at **6' Palio Espresso & Dessert House,** a cozily romantic coffee shop and cafe right across the street from the neighborhood's central park garden. Stumptown coffee and plenty of different teas are served in a setting that feels a bit like an antique bookstore. *1996 SE Ladd Ave.* ☎ *503/232-9412. $.*

6 ★ **kids** **Laurelhurst Park.** In the mood for more park rambling? Thank former mayor William Ladd (see Ladd's Addition, above) and the famous Olmsted Brothers landscape design firm for this 26-acre park in the neighborhood of the same name (Laurelhurst). Grand old trees shade paved trails, picnic tables, and open lawns, including an off-leash area for dogs; it is most definitely one of the city's prettiest parks. Originally a spring-fed pond, 3-acre Firwood Lake was dredged in 2011 and fitted with a water circulation and aeration system. The lawn next to it is the best spot on the east side to lounge away a sunny Friday afternoon. A smaller "play park" section between SE Oak and Stark streets has tennis courts, a soccer field, a playground, bathrooms, and a small dance studio for public recreation classes. ⏱ *30 min. Btw. SE 33rd & 39th aves., Oak & Ankeny sts. Open daily 5am–10:30pm. Bus: 75.*

8 ★ **Mount Tabor.** If you're eager for more rugged outdoorsy

Smoke jumper simulator in the World Forestry Center Discovery Museum.

PDX Playlist

Seattle and L.A. may get more press, but Portland has been home to outstanding live music ever since The Kingsmen garbled their way through "Louie, Louie" in one take in 1963. (After a 2-year obscenity investigation, the FBI concluded the song was "unintelligible at any speed.") Here's the perfect soundtrack of local, or at least once-local, artists for your visit.

- "Louie, Louie," The Kingsmen, 1963
- "I Can't Wait," Nu Shooz, *Poolside*, 1986
- "Ride," Dandy Warhols, *Dandys Rule, OK?* 1995
- "I Will Buy You A New Life," Everclear, *So Much For the Afterglow*, 1997
- "Between the Bars," Elliott Smith, *Either/Or*, 1997
- "Light Rail Coyote," Sleater-Kinney, *One Beat*, 2002
- "Phantom Limb," The Shins, *Chutes Too Narrow*, 2003
- "Let's Never Stop Falling in Love," Pink Martini, *Hang On Little Tomato*, 2004
- "On The Bus Mall," The Decemberists, *Picaresque*, 2005
- "People Say," Portugal. The Man, *The Satanic Satanist*, 2009

action, venture out to this 190-acre city park. How many cities in the continental U.S. can boast an extinct volcano within their city limits? Only two, actually, and they're both in Oregon: Bend and Portland. The 630-foot-high cinder cone of Portland's Mount Tabor is topped by three open reservoirs (recently disconnected from the water system but still used as a "water feature"). Its forests are laced with trails for bikers and hikers, and near a large playground, an amphitheater hosts free outdoor concerts on Tuesday evenings in the summer. *Open daily 5am–10pm, closed to motor vehicles Wed. Enter at SE Salmon St. & 60th Ave., SE Lincoln & 64th Ave., SE Yamhill & 69th Ave., or SE Harrison St. & 71st Ave. Bus: 4, 15, or 71.* ●

Portland with Kids

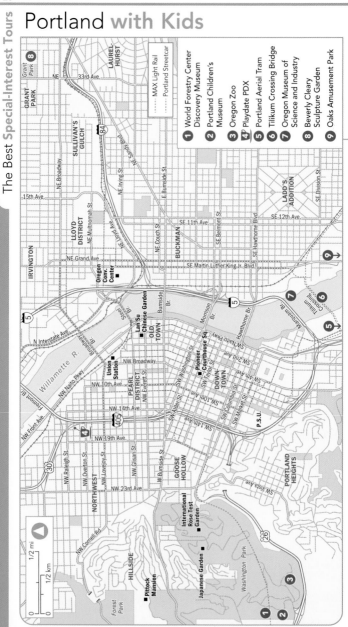

····· MAX Light Rail
---- Portland Streetcar

1 World Forestry Center Discovery Museum
2 Portland Children's Museum
3 Oregon Zoo
4 Playdate PDX
5 Portland Aerial Tram
6 Tilikum Crossing Bridge
7 Oregon Museum of Science and Industry
8 Beverly Cleary Sculpture Garden
9 Oaks Amusement Park

Previous page: The Lan Su Chinese Garden on a rainy day.

Portland repeatedly gets voted one of the best cities in the country to raise kids. Certain neighborhoods, especially on the east side, are full of couples with children, and there are days when it seems that strollers and baby backpacks are almost as ubiquitous as bikes in the city's parks and on its sidewalks. Kids love Portland's wealth of bridges, trails, and rivers, and there are plenty of activities right in town to keep them busy, including the sites adjacent to each other in Washington Park. START: **MAX to Washington Park. Bus 63 on weekdays.**

A bridge through the tree canopy at the World Forestry Center Discovery Museum.

1 World Forestry Center Discovery Museum. At this paean to all things arboreal, two floors of interactive displays give kids (and their attendant grown-ups) some real insight into the importance of the Northwest's majestic stands of forest. Kids especially love the virtual smokejumper and river-rafting exhibits—and after a visit here they'll be

ready to dive into the real forests of Washington Park right outside the museum's doors. *See p 22, bullet 3.*

2 ★★ Portland Children's Museum. Right next door to the World Forestry Center Discovery Museum, also in Washington Park, is a castle of creativity and fun, one of the oldest children's musems in the country. The displays are constantly updated—and hands-on, of course—including exhibits themed around popular characters like Curious George and Clifford the Big Red Dog. Kids age 10 and under can burrow in the rubber gravel of the Dig Pit, sculpt a city in the Clay Studio, build something in the Garage, or take the stage at the Play It Again Theater. A stop at the Water Works will probably require a change of clothes, but it's worth it. The Baby's Garden caters to tots under 3. A varying schedule of classes and story times keeps things fresh. *Note:* The museum can get crowded at peak times, so consider coming on weekday late afternoons, after all the school groups have left. ⏱ 1½ hr. 4015 SW Canyon Rd. ☎ 503/223-6500. www.portlandcm.org. Open daily 9am–5pm, Thurs until 8pm; free 1st Friday of every month 4–8pm. Admission $11 ages 1–54, $9.75 over 54, free under 1. MAX: Washington Park. Bus: 63 on weekdays only.

Fun at the Portland Children's Museum.

③ ★★ Oregon Zoo. It's hard to decide which animals children like best here: the frolicking river otters, the powerful Amur tigers, the acrobatic chimpanzees, or the naked mole rats. In any case, the miniature train is a sure-fire favorite, circling the zoo and venturing off into the rest of Washington Park. Come early or stay late to increase your odds of seeing animals in action. *See p 15, bullet* **②**.

At **④ Playdate PDX's** 7,500-square-foot indoor playground, you can enjoy a panini and coffee while your progeny run wild on a multistory castle with ropes, swings, and slides. Admission isn't cheap—$8 to $12 per kid, $4 to $6 ages 3 and under—and it can get packed; but on a rainy day it's a real stress-reducer. *1434 NW 17th Ave.* ☎ *503/227-7529. www.playdate pdx.com. Daily 9am–8pm. $.*

⑤ Portland Aerial Tram. A fun trip to the hospital? Yes, when it involves a ride in a space-age pod that sails ⅔ of a mile (and 500 ft. up) from Oregon Health Science University's Center for Health & Healing at South Waterfront to the main OHSU campus up on Marquam Hill (also known as Pill Hill). On nice days, the $57-million tram offers views of Mt. Hood, Mt. St. Helens, and, of course, the river and downtown. ⏱ *30 min. Departs every 6–10 min. Lower terminal and ticket kiosk at 3303 SW Bond Ave. www.gobytram.com. Admission $4.50 round-trip, children 6 and under free. Mon–Fri 5:30am–9:30pm; Sat (May–Sept only) 9am–5pm; Sun 1–5pm; closed major holidays. Streetcar: OHSU Commons. Bus: 35 or 36.*

Birds-eye views from the Portland Aerial Tram.

Outdoor Fountains

In the heat of the summer, the irony of cavorting in water in such a damp city evaporates like puddles on concrete, and kids pack Portland's many public water fountains. Even if it's too cool or cloudy to splash, they're still fun to see. Just don't take a drink; they all use chlorinated, recycled water. Fountains generally flow from spring through fall.

Ira Keller Fountain. If you can't make it up the Columbia Gorge, this fountain in the heart of downtown is the closest you'll come to a waterfall: an abstract rock face of edges and drop-offs spilling 75,000 gallons of water. Too steep and slippery for climbing, this fountain is more for visual enjoyment and wading. *SW 3rd Ave. & SW Clay St.*

Jamison Square Fountain. One of Portland's most popular hot-weather destinations fills half a block in the Pearl District. The shallow wading pool is geared toward toddlers and babies, while older kids can clamber up the steps of the cascades. The other half of the park consists of grass and trees for lounging in the shade. *NW 11th Ave. & Johnson St.*

Bill Naito Legacy Fountain. Actually two fountains at one end of Waterfront Park's new Portland Saturday Market plaza, this small amphitheater features a series of water arches and a flat plaza under a glass roof with dozens of vertical jet "blow-holes." The latter is turned off and filled with vendors during the market. *SW Naito Pkwy. & SW Ankeny St., in Governor Tom McCall Waterfront Park.*

Salmon Street Springs. The most distinctive and impressive of the city's fountains anchors the southern end of Governor Tom McCall Waterfront Park. Concentric circles of 185 jets spout water in every imaginable pattern, controlled by an underground computer that changes the pattern every 20 minutes. Almost 5,000 gallons of water a minute gush at peak volume—so older toddlers, grade-schoolers, and pre-teens will enjoy it most. *SW Naito Pkwy. & SW Salmon St. in Governor Tom McCall Waterfront Park.*

Teachers Fountain. The newest public square downtown, dedicated to educators, has a gentle fountain with low jets and burbles feeding into a shallow pool ringed by benches. *SW Yamhill & SW Park aves.*

6 ★★ Tilikum Crossing Bridge. Right next to the aerial tram, catch the newest extension of the Portland Streetcar (A Loop) and take a ride over the Willamette River via the city's brand-new Tilikum Crossing Bridge, which opened in 2015. The distinctive cable-stayed "Bridge of the People" is the first in the country designed exclusively for pedestrians, light-rail, streetcar, and bicycles only. (No cars allowed.) You can also walk across and pick up the streetcar to OMSI on the other side; along the way you'll enjoy some great views west toward downtown. ⏱ *30 minutes. Streetcars depart every 15–20 min. Streetcar: A Loop from OHSU Commons. Fares: adults $2, seniors/ages 7–17 $1.25.*

7 ★ Oregon Museum of Science and Industry. From the Omnimax dome theater to the submarine docked in the Willamette, the earthquake simulator and the pint-size science playroom for kids 6 and under, OMSI is 219,000 square feet of interactive learning and educational fun. *See p 67, bullet 2.*

8 Beverly Cleary Sculpture Garden. Fans of the famous children's author will find statues of three of her most beloved characters—Henry Huggins, Ramona Quimby, and Henry's dog, Ribsy—in Grant Park, which appears in several of her books. The statues are just south of the playground near Grant High School, which Cleary also wrote about. Across 33rd Street, the grade school she attended as a child now bears her name. (In the public library branch at NE Tillamook and 40th Ave., a large map of the neighborhood marks more local landmarks in her books.) ⏱ *15 min. NE Brazee St. & NE 33rd Ave. Bus: 73.*

9 ★★ Oaks Amusement Park. A fun-filled time warp on the bank of the Willamette River near Sellwood, Oaks Amusement Park opened in 1905 to accompany the Lewis and Clark Centennial Exposition. The oldest continually operating amusement park in the country,

The new Tilikum Crossing Bridge.

The Beverly Cleary Sculpture Garden.

it has two dozen modern rides, including the Scream-n-Eagle and the Looping Thunder Roller Coaster, along with classics like a Ferris wheel, a Tilt-a-Whirl, go-karts, and a miniature train that chugs along the waterfront. Nostalgists appreciate the 1912 carved carousel, midway games, and wooden roller- and ice-skating rink with a suspended pipe organ. There's no charge to enter the park and use its picnic grounds, where a path leads down the bluff to the river's edge. ⏱ *2 hr. 7805 SE Oaks Park Way.* ☎ *503/233-5777. www. oakspark.com. Hours vary. Rides usually Mar–Oct Sat & Sun noon–7pm; June–Aug Tues–Sun noon–9pm. Skating rink open year-round Tues–Sun in afternoon and evening sessions. Free admission to grounds; ride tickets $2.50 each, unlimited ride bracelets $13–$16, go-karts $5 driver, $2 passengers, skating $6.50–$7.75, skate rental $2.50–$6. Bus: 70.*

The Best Special-Interest Tours

Offbeat Portland

1 Peculiarium & Museum
2 Zoobomb Monument
3 Pioneer Courthouse Square
4 Voodoo Doughnut
5 Mill Ends Park
6 Stark's Vaccuum Museum
7 Rimsky-Korsakoffee House
8 Kidd's Toy Museum
9 The Hat Museum
10 Mike's Museum of Motion Picture History

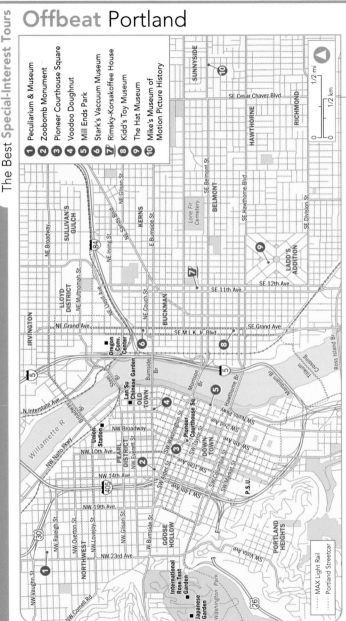

MAX Light Rail
Portland Streetcar

❚❚Keep Portland Weird" isn't just a ubiquitous local bumper sticker; here it's a way of life. Whether it's the long cloudy winters or the concentration of creative types (or both), Portland has a streak of strange it wears proudly. There's plenty here to amuse your inner oddball, from one-of-a-kind museums to kooky and chaotic annual events. START: **Bus 17 to NW Thurman Ave. & 22nd Pl.**

❶ ★ **Peculiarium & Museum.**
Part museum, part art gallery, part gift shop, and part ice-cream parlor, the Peculiarium lives up to its name. Here you'll find skulls, vampire-killing kits, and a 10-foot Sasquatch, just for starters. There's an interactive alien autopsy and a motel room painted entirely in glow-in-the-dark paint, plus changing exhibits on things like spontaneous human combustion. The in-house magician sometimes gives lessons and live shows. Finish off your visit with something from the ice-cream bar, but be warned: The Bug-Eater's Delight is not a descriptive metaphor. ⏱ *30 min. 2234 NW Thurman St.* ☎ *503/227-3164. www.peculiarium.com. $5 for all; dogs in costume get in free. Open Thurs–Sun 11am–6pm. Bus: 17.*

❷ ★ **Zoobomb monument.**
One of the proudest and definitely most unusual traditions in this bike-mad city is the weekly Sunday

Weird but true: the Zoobomb monument.

The wacky Peculiarium & Museum.

evening ride—and I use the term loosely—from the zoo down the West Hills. It's the strangest peloton you've ever seen, full of tall bikes, kids' bikes (ridden by adults), skateboards, and essentially anything wheeled and human-powered. Some riders dress in outlandish costumes, and everyone has a blast. If you don't have your own bike, don't worry: Outside the American Apparel store at 13th Avenue and West Burnside Street is a monument (read: pile on a pole) of bikes, including some spares, chained up and waiting for Sunday night. A gold-plated minibike tops the public artwork, also known as the "People's Bike Library of Portland." Zoobomb riders meet here every Sunday around 8:30pm. Bring a bike if you have one, as well as a helmet, MAX fare, and lights. ① *15 min. 13th St. & West Burnside Ave. www.zoobomb.net. Bus: 20.*

❸ ★ kids **Pioneer Courthouse Square.** The most trafficked block in the city still has a few tricks up its sleeves. Throughout the plaza are bricks engraved with the names of donors who helped fund the space—or pseudonyms. See if you can find Mr. Spock, Sherlock Holmes, Jesus Christ, and Bilbo Baggins. (You can order your own for $100.) The small amphitheater in the northwest corner, below the bronze chess boards, is an echo chamber; if you stand on the central marble stone and speak, it creates a huge echo that only you can hear. Next to the amphitheater is a pole-mounted weather machine. A series of lights show the temperature, and every day at noon, a fanfare announces the weather prediction, indicated by an icon that pops out of the globe on top: a heron for light rain, a dragon for heavy rain, and a sun for, well, sun. On the 6th Avenue side of the plaza, a milepost indicates the distance to places like Mt. Hood, Moscow, Timbuktu, and Tipperary ("a long way"). *See p 9, bullet ❶.*

Shanghai Tunnels

In the late 19th century, when Portland was the second-biggest port on the West Coast, miles of underground tunnels were built to move goods from the riverside docks into the city. Unfortunately, they were also used to kidnap thousands of drunks and transients from bars, brothels, and boardinghouses to press into service on large sailing ships. Hired thugs used opium knockout drops and trapdoors to grab their prey, receiving payment for each warm body they delivered. At its peak, Portland was said to lead the world in the practice, called *Shanghaiing* because victims often woke up at sea on ships headed to Asia. The tunnels were sealed in 1941, but you can tour them today with Portland Walking Tours (☎ 503/774-4522; **www.portlandwalkingtours.com**). Tours meet outside Old Merchant Hotel at 131 NW 2nd Ave. (at Davis St.) at 11am and 2pm daily April to November; December to March Friday and Saturday. The tour costs $20 adults, $17 seniors 65 and over and youth 11 to 17, $9 children 5 to 10.

The gigantic Texas Challenge doughnut at Voodoo Doughnuts.

4 ★ Mill Ends Park. Portland isn't just home to one of the largest urban parks (Forest Park) in the country; it also boasts the world's smallest, a patch of flowers 24 inches across in the median of SW Naito Parkway at Taylor Street. It started in 1948 when a newspaper journalist, whose office overlooked the road, planted flowers and began writing whimsical columns about a leprechaun named Patrick O'Toole who lived there with his family. It was formally recognized as a city park in 1976—on St. Patrick's Day, of course. *MAX: Yamhill District. Bus: 15 or 51.*

5 ★ kids Voodoo Doughnut. If one place embodies Portland's culture of comestible eccentricity, it's this Old Town eatery where the art of deep-fried pastry circles is taken to new extremes. Doughnuts crusted with Cap'n Crunch and Fruit Loops sit next to Bacon Maple Bars (topped with real bacon) and the person-shaped Voodoo Doll, filled with raspberry jelly and impaled on a pretzel. If you can eat the giant Texas Challenge in under 80 seconds, it's free. Open 24 hours, Voodoo is popular with late-night revelers, and you can some-times catch live music or a real live wedding going on, catered with (what else?) coffee and doughnuts. A second location opened in 2011 at 1501 NE Davis St., complete with a bridge-crossing ceremony to transport the hallowed deep-frying oil. ⏲ *30 min. 22 SW 3rd Ave.* ☎ *503/241-4704. www.voodoo doughnut.com. Open 24 hr. MAX: Skidmore Fountain. Bus: 12, 19, or 20.*

6 ★ Stark's Vacuum Museum. Did you know they made vacuums out of cardboard during the Great Depression? You will after a visit to this display of powered cleaners through the ages, part of Stark's Vacuum Cleaner Sales & Service. Most of the 300 models were donated by locals, including hand-pumped ones from the 19th century (includ-ing one that took two people to operate) and retro-futuristic models from the space-age '60s. Careful—you might just be inspired to leave with a modern Hoover or Dyson. ⏲ *30 min. 107 NE Grand Ave.* ☎ *800/230-4101. www.starks.com. Free admission. Open Mon–Fri 8am–7pm; Sat 9am–5pm; Sun 11am–5pm. Bus: 6, 2, 19, or 20.*

The most atmospheric coffeehouse in town, and one of the oldest, **7 Rimsky-Korsakoffee House** fills a former Victorian home with oddball art, moving tables, and decorated bathrooms you have to see to believe. The waiters are fun and sassy and the desserts, especially the sundaes, to die for. Some say the place is actually haunted. *707 SE 12th Ave.* ☎ *503/232-2640. $.*

Top things off at the Hat Museum.

8 ★ Kidd's Toy Museum. Fans of antique playthings will love this private collection of hundreds, if not thousands, of toys, games, banks, and other trinkets dating as far back as the 1850s. Frank Kidd has filled one section of his auto parts warehouse with row upon row of vintage trains, soldiers, cars, and trucks. His mechanical cast-iron banks are worth a museum in themselves, with models that show a dentist extracting a tooth or kids peeking at a bathing beauty. (Parent alert: Some items are quite un-PC by modern standards.) Nothing is labeled, not even the building—look for a paper sign taped to the door—but Frank, who's often on site, can give you details on just about anything in his singular collection, which includes dolls and teddy bears his wife has collected. ⏱ *1 hr. 1301 SE Grand Ave.* ☎ *503/233-7807. Free admission. Hours are officially Mon–Thurs noon–6pm; Fri 1–6pm; weekends by appt. Bus: 6.*

9 ★ The Hat Museum. One of the country's largest collections of headgear fills a 1910 home in Ladd's Addition, once the home of a talented hatmaker. Over 1,300 hats for men and women, from antique Stetsons to modern tea hats, make up five distinct collections that span the globe. The tour (required) by owner Alyce Cornyn-Selby includes a wealth of detail on the history of hats and their creation, plus a $5 credit toward anything in the gift shop. Don't miss the novelty models, like the Thanksgiving table hat that sings and others that fold or hide things inside. The house itself is a curiosity, with secret spaces, mermaid ceiling paintings, and a couch made from a 1966 Cadillac. ⏱ *1½ hr. 1928 SE Ladd Ave.* ☎ *503/232-0433. www. thehatmuseum.com. Daily 10am–6pm. Tours required, $5 for groups of 1 to 6 by prior appointment only. Bus: 10.*

10 ★ Mike's Museum of Motion Picture History. Film buffs know that Movie Madness is the best place in town to find videos and DVDs of classic, independent, and cult movies. It's also home to a collection of costumes and props from famous films, like the baby carriage from the stairway shootout in *The Untouchables* and an alien creature from *Mars Attacks*. Look for Julie Andrews' dress from *The Sound of Music* and Orson Welles's jacket from *Touch of Evil*, a classic 1958 film noir. ⏱ *45 min. 4320 SE Belmont St.* ☎ *503/234-4363. www.moviemadnessvideo.com/museum. Daily 11am–11pm. Free admission. Bus: 15.*

Odd Events

At certain times of year, Portland's peculiarity spikes with annual events that celebrate the eccentric in each of us. On the first Saturday in March, the **Urban Iditarod** replaces huskies with people, sleds with shopping carts, and 1,000 miles through Alaska's frigid wastes with a 4-mile route across downtown Portland. (The event was cancelled in 2015, but never say die; it might occur again.) Outlandish costumes are the rule and everyone's a winner. In mid-June, the 2-week annual bike festival known as Pedalpalooza includes Portland's contribution to the **World Naked Bike Ride,** consisting of thousands—that's right, *thousands*—of unclothed riders taking a lighthearted (and often chilly) spin around town. As seen below, the mid-August **PDX Adult Soapbox Derby** (www.soapboxracer.com) updates the classic gravity cars of childhood with PhD-level engineering, museum-quality art, and lots of beer. More than 5,000 people gather on the slopes of Mt. Tabor to watch cars hit speeds of over 50 mph, competing for prizes in decoration, velocity, and crowd-pleasing.

If you happen to see a large group of boisterous Santas careening around town in early December, chances are it's the latest incarnation of **SantaCon** (www.pdxcacophony.org), a mix of holiday spirit, performance art, and inebriated rowdiness organized by the Portland Cacophony Society (motto: "Life is short. Mess with someone else's.").

The Adult Soapbox Derby.

Rainy Day Portland

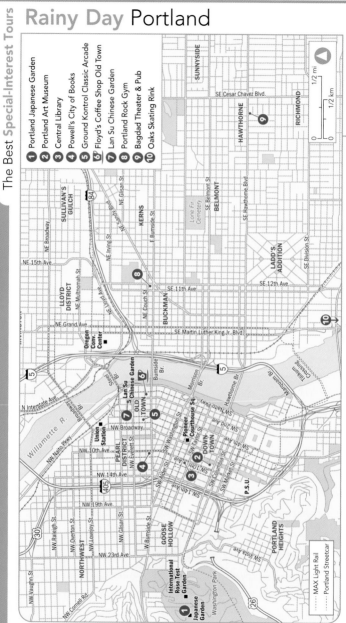

1 Portland Japanese Garden
2 Portland Art Museum
3 Central Library
4 Powell's City of Books
5 Ground Kontrol Classic Arcade
6 Floyd's Coffee Shop Old Town
7 Lan Su Chinese Garden
8 Portland Rock Gym
9 Bagdad Theater & Pub
10 Oaks Skating Rink

MAX Light Rail
Portland Streetcar

It's a fact of life: from fall through spring, and especially in the winter, Portland gets a lot of rain. (More than famously wet Seattle does, in fact.) But that doesn't mean there still isn't plenty to do when the clouds roll in and the misty Northwest drizzle starts. Most of the activities on this tour are indoors, for obvious reasons, but a few outdoor ones take advantage of the moody change in atmosphere overcast skies can bring. So get out your rubber boots and rain jackets—Portlanders are notoriously averse to umbrellas—and head out. START: **MAX to Washington Park. Bus 63 on weekdays.**

Browsing the galleries of the Portland Art Museum.

❶ ★★★ Portland Japanese Garden. Washington Park's world-class Japanese garden is just as enchanting—maybe more—in the rain as it is in the sun. Like most classical Japanese gardens, it's designed with the changing seasons in mind, with certain scenes best viewed in the rain (or snow, for that matter). The rough stones, meticulously trimmed shrubs, and placid koi pond take on a different, yet still serene, atmosphere of dripping leaves and rippling water. Just take care with some of the rock steps—they get very slippery. *See p 15, bullet* **❶**.

❷ ★ Portland Art Museum. Spend an hour indoors drying off with Marcel Duchamp, Gustave Courbet, Albert Bierstadt, and Ansel Adams—or at least their works—at Portland's best-known art institution. Time it right to catch a free gallery tour, lecture, or Midday Art Break. *Tours Sun–Fri 12:30pm and occasionally in the afternoon. See p 10, bullet* **❸**.

❸ ★ kids Central Library. The main branch of the Multnomah County Library, opened in 1913, fills a massive Georgian-style building downtown with 875 *tons* of books on over 17 miles of bookshelves. Just stepping inside is inspiring, with the sweeping main staircase climbing through a three-story atrium. The **Beverly Cleary**

Children's Library, named after the famous local author, has a sculpture of Alice in Wonderland and a 14-foot bronze tree covered in carved images from kids' books like *The Wizard of Oz* and *The Little Engine That Could.* On the third floor, the **Collins Gallery** hosts rotating art exhibits, and the **John Wilson Special Collections** focus on Pacific Northwest history, children's literature, and Native American books. ○ *1 hr. 801 SW 10th Ave.* ☎ *503/988-5123. www.multcolib.org. Mon, Thurs & Sat 10am–6pm; Tues & Wed 10am–8pm; Sun noon–5pm. Streetcar: A & B Loop. MAX: Library/SW 9th Ave.*

❹ ★★★ **kids** **Powell's City of Books.** Satisfy any lingering literary cravings at Portland's world-class independent bookseller. Browse through 3,500 sections, including an outstanding **children's section** in the first-floor Rose Room. The **Basil Hallward Gallery,** upstairs in the Pearl Room, hosts new art exhibits every month, and the **World Cup coffee shop** has plenty of seats for browsing and watching the rain fall through the windowed walls. *See p 77.*

❺ ★ **kids** **Ground Kontrol Classic Arcade.** If you spent a good chunk of your childhood weekends in video arcades, this two-story retro game room will whisk you back to the days of honing your skills at Centipede and Donkey Kong. Ground Kontrol has more than 90 cabinet games from the past 40 years, from oldies like Asteroids and Tempest to the newest, like the four-player Pac-Man Battle Royale. And they're all still only a quarter! Get a workout on Dance Dance Revolution in the back corner, or head upstairs for dozens of pinball machines. A full bar serves drinks and snacks, and DJs spin music in the evenings. Every second Thursday and last Wednesday evening of the month, admission is $5 and all games are

Pinball machines at Ground Kontrol Classic Arcade.

The Lan Su Chinese Garden changes moods with the weather.

free. ⏲ 45 min. 511 NW Couch St. ☎ 503/796-9364. www.ground kontrol.com. Free admission. Daily noon–2:30am, ages 21 and over only after 5pm. MAX: NW 5th & Couch St.

Serving Stumptown coffee in the ambiance of an old diner, ⑥ **Floyd's Coffee Shop Old Town** (there's another one on the East Side) has comfy seating, inexpensive eats, and outstanding espresso drinks, perfect for a respite from the drizzle. 118 NW Couch St. ☎ 503/295-7791. MAX: Old Town/Chinatown. Bus: 12, 19, 20. $.

❼ ★★★ **Lan Su Chinese Garden.** Like the Portland Japanese Garden (see p 39), this leafy escape in the heart of Chinatown was designed to be appreciated in any kind of weather. Covered walkways lead between ornate pavilions with names like "Painted Boat in Misty Rain" and "Flowers Bathing in Spring Rain." Banana plants are positioned under rain gutters to create a distinctive sound when splashed with water. The Chinese Garden is a peaceful place to spend a damp afternoon, particularly the teahouse, where you can linger over a pot of lapsang souchong and contemplate the central lake. *See p 17, bullet* ❸.

❽ ★ **Portland Rock Gym.** Rock climbing in the rain? Sure, when it's inside the state's largest rock gym. Walls 35 feet high are studded with artificial climbing holds, offering an ever-changing selection of 100 climbing routes of all levels, each flagged with colored tape. In case you've never climbed before, they offer instruction and gear rental, as well as a weight room, cardio machines, and yoga and Pilates classes. Ropes are mandatory in the main room, but in the bouldering area you can learn this low-level skill (you're never more than a few feet off the padded floor) without being "tied in." Experts can tackle the 16-foot overhang or dozens of lead-climbing routes. ⏲ 1 hr. 21 NE 12th Ave. ☎ 503/232-8310. www.portlandrockgym.com. Open Mon, Wed, Fri 11am–11pm; Tues &

Thurs 7am–11pm; Sat 9am–9pm; Sun 9am–6pm. Day pass $17 adults ($12 before 3pm Mon–Fri), $12 children 11 and under, $9 seniors 62 and older on weekdays. Bus: 12, 19, 20, or 70.

9 ★ kids Bagdad Theater & Pub. Sometimes all you want to do on an overcast evening is eat pizza, drink beer, and watch a movie. This proud artifact of the Golden Age of Hollywood lets you do it in a little style. Built by Universal Pictures in 1927 for $100,000, it survived the transition from vaudeville to "talkies" and hosted everyone from Sammy Davis, Jr., to Jack Nicholson and Michael Douglas, here for the 1975 premiere of *One Flew Over the Cuckoo's Nest.* Since taking over the property in the early 1990s, the McMenamin brothers have restored the movie palace to all its faux–Middle Eastern glory, including wrought-iron fixtures, tiled arches, and paintings. The pub serves pizza, burgers, and hand-crafted ales, all of which you can bring into the theater for movies and the occasional comedy show or author reading. (Don't miss the Backstage Bar behind the screen, with its seven-story ceiling.) ◷ *1–2 hr. 3702 SE Hawthorne Blvd.* ☎ *503/467-7521. www.mcmenamins. com/bagdad. Tickets $2–$28. Pub open Mon–Thurs 11am–midnight, Fri & Sat 11am–1am, Sun noon–midnight. Backstage Bar open*

Vintage roller-skating rink at Oaks Amusement Park.

Mon–Thurs 5pm–midnight, Fri 5pm–2:30am, Sat 2pm–2:30am, Sun 2pm–midnight. Bus: 14.

10 ★ kids Oaks Amusement Park Skating Rink. The weather is an afterthought inside the wooden skating rink at Oaks Amusement Park, open (like the park itself) since 1905. It's a roll through the halls of nostalgia, circling the lovingly maintained floor beneath the working Wurlitzer pipe organ. You can rent skates, grab a snack, and even take a lesson on weekends. See p 71, bullet **3**. ●

Downtown Portland

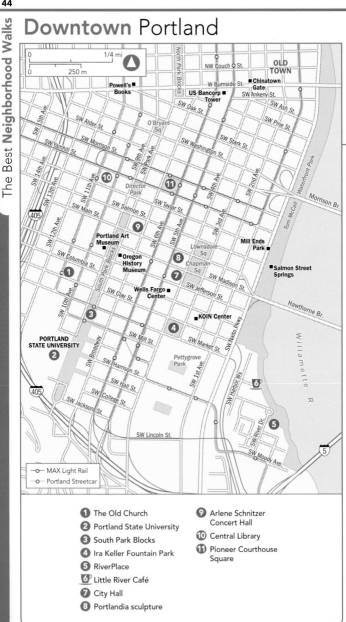

0 ——— 1/4 mi
0 ——— 250 m

North Park Blocks

NW Couch St.
OLD TOWN
W Burnside St.
Chinatown Gate
SW Ankeny St.
SW Ash St.
SW Pine St.
SW Stark St.

Powell's Books
US Bancorp Tower
SW Oak St.
SW Washington St.

SW 5th Ave.
SW Alder St.
SW Morrison St.
SW Yamhill St.
O'Bryant Sq.
SW 9th Ave.
SW Park Ave.
SW 4th Ave.

SW 15th Ave.
SW 14th Ave.
SW 13th Ave.
SW 12th Ave.
SW 11th Ave.
405

⑩
Director Park
⑪
SW Taylor St.
SW Salmon St.
SW Main St.
SW 6th Ave.
SW 5th Ave.
SW 3rd Ave.
SW 2nd Ave.
Morrison Br.
Waterfront Park
Tom McCall

⑨
Portland Art Museum
Oregon History Museum
South Park Blocks
SW Columbia St.
SW Clay St.
①
③
SW 10th Ave.
Lownsdale Sq.
⑧
Chapman Sq.
⑦
Wells Fargo Center
SW Madison St.
SW Jefferson St.
Mill Ends Park
Salmon Street Springs
Willamette R.

■ KOIN Center
④
SW Market St.
Hawthorne Br.

PORTLAND STATE UNIVERSITY
②
SW Broadway
SW Mill St.
SW Harrison St.
Pettygrove Park
SW 1st Ave.
SW Naito Pkwy.
SW Harbor Wy.

SW Hall St.
SW College St.
405
SW Jackson St.
⑥
⑤
SW River Dr.
SW Moody Ave.

SW Lincoln St.
5

—o— MAX Light Rail
—o— Portland Streetcar

1 The Old Church
2 Portland State University
3 South Park Blocks
4 Ira Keller Fountain Park
5 RiverPlace
6 Little River Café
7 City Hall
8 Portlandia sculpture

9 Arlene Schnitzer Concert Hall
10 Central Library
11 Pioneer Courthouse Square

Previous page: The St. John's Bridge rises over Northwest Portland.

Downtown Portland is surprisingly compact and manageable for the heart of the state's largest city. Busy as it may be, it's still possible to walk from one end to the other in 30 minutes or less. Along with a mass of offices and government buildings, downtown is home to Oregon's largest university (Portland State) as well as plenty of shops, restaurants, and cultural venues to keep you entertained. Alternatives to walking or biking are the MAX light rail, buses, or the streetcar. START: **Streetcar at SW 11th & Clay, bus: 6, 43, 45, 55, 58, or 68.**

The Ira Keller Fountain evokes Northwest mountain waterfalls.

❶ ★ **The Old Church.** Built of wood in a style known as Carpenter Gothic, this ornate Victorian beauty started as a Presbyterian church in 1883, making it one of the oldest buildings in the Pacific Northwest. Today it's owned by a nonprofit organization and hosts music concerts and other public events. Many of the original architectural features have been preserved, including hand-carved fir pews and built-in umbrella racks. ⏱ *15 min. 1422 SW 11th Ave.* ☎ *503/222-2031. www. oldchurch.org. Open Mon–Fri 11am–3pm. Self-guided tours are free; admission varies by scheduled event.*

❷ ★ **Portland State University.** With 30,000 students, the largest university in Oregon anchors the southern end of downtown with its leafy 49-acre urban campus. A large percentage of the student body is older—the average age for undergrads is around 25—and many classes meet in the evenings and on weekends. ⏱ *15 min. Btw. SW Market St, SW 3rd Ave. & I-405.* ☎ *503/725-3000. www.pdx.edu.*

❸ ★ **South Park Blocks.** Thank Portland cofounder Daniel Lownsdale for this strip of 12 grassy blocks leading from the PSU campus into the center of downtown. Four years after buying up most of what would become downtown Portland in 1848, Lownsdale donated the land to the city (some say, to guard his property from forest fires). ⏱ *30 min. SW Park Ave. btw. Salmon & Hall sts. Open daily*

❹ ★ **kids Ira Keller Fountain Park.** When this urban park and waterfall designed by famed San Francisco architect Lawrence Halprin was unveiled in 1970, *New York Times* architectural critic Ada Louise Huxtable hailed it "the greatest public fountain since the Renaissance." Maybe that's overdoing it, but the fountain has stood the test of time. Its design, with pools, streams, stepping stones, and tall vertical planes (all made of concrete) is meant to evoke Oregon's many mountain waterfalls. It's designed so you can walk to the top and look over (there's a 3-foot lip hidden under the water at the edge). ⏱ *15 min. SW 3rd Ave. & SW Clay St.*

⑤ ★ **RiverPlace.** Portland's urban downtown meets its lifeblood river here at this modern 50-acre development between the noisy Marquam (I-5) and Hawthorne bridges. RiverPlace combines condos, townhomes, shops, and a hotel with a public marina and a popular riverbank park; an extension of the riverfront pedestrian esplanade leads past a row of shops and restaurants that are packed with people on sunny afternoons. ⏱ *1 hr. Btw. SW Harbor Way & SW Montgomery St. Streetcar: SW River Pkwy & Moody.*

Tasty soups and sandwiches are the order of the day at the snug ⑥ **Little River Café** in the middle of the RiverPlace esplanade. There's not much space inside, but the outside seats are great for watching local "dragonboats" paddle up and down the river. *315 SW Montgomery St. #310.* ☎ *503/227-2327. www. littlerivercafe.com. Hours vary with season; in summer 7am–8:30pm Mon–Thurs, 7am–9pm Fri–Sun. $.*

⑦ ★ **City Hall.** Built in 1895, the home of Portland's City Council underwent a full renovation in the 1990s, restoring the four-story Italianate building to its original glory. Commissioned artworks, both permanent and temporary, decorate the interior. ⏱ *15 min. 1221 SW 4th Ave.* ☎ *503/823-4000. www.portland online.com. Mon–Fri. 9am–4pm.*

⑧ ★★ **Portlandia sculpture.** Before there was *Portlandia* the TV series, there was Portlandia the sculpture: the nation's second-largest hammered-copper statue, after the Statue of Liberty. Based on the city seal, the 34-foot-high "Lady Commerce," installed in 1985, kneels over the entrance to Michael Graves' ugly and much-despised

Pioneer Courthouse Square is a prime spot for people-watching.

Benson Bubblers

In 1912, a local lumber baron, philanthropist, and teetotaler named Simon Benson noticed that his mill workers' breath smelled like booze. Upon learning that fresh water was hard to find downtown, Benson donated $10,000 to the city to install 20 bronze drinking fountains. (His ploy worked: Beer consumption allegedly fell 25%.) There are now 52 "Benson bubblers" throughout Portland, mostly downtown, including the original four-bowl fountain at SW 5th Avenue and Washington Street. (Another 74 single-bowl versions were added later.) They're cleaned regularly and flow daily with fresh Bull Run drinking water.

One of the many Benson Bubbler drinking fountains around downtown.

postmodern Portland Building, holding a trident in one hand and reaching down with the other. *1120 SW 5th Ave. btw. Madison & Main sts.*

⑨ ★ Arlene Schnitzer Concert Hall. The most historic of the three properties that make up the Portland Center for the Performing Arts, "the Schnitz," as it's known locally, is the last of the grand old theaters that once lined Broadway. Built in 1928, it was a vaudeville house and movie theater before being restored in 1984 to its original Hollywood Moorish splendor. The distinctive 65-foot "Portland" sign outside is lit with more than 5,000 lights. The superlative Oregon Symphony and the White Bird Dance Company perform here, along with various art programs and lectures. *1037 SW Broadway at

Main St.* ☎ *503/248-4335. www. pcpa.com. Ticket prices and show-times vary.*

⑩ ★ kids Central Library. There's something for everyone at the Multnomah County Library's main branch, a Georgian-style building with a sweeping central staircase, three-story atrium, and cozy children's library. *See p 39, bullet ③.*

⑪ ★★ kids Pioneer Court-house Square. Shoemaker Elijah Hill purchased this downtown block in 1849 for $24 and a pair of high boots. Since then it's hosted the city's first school, the second-oldest federal courthouse in the West (the 1875 Pioneer Courthouse, still standing, for which the square is named), and, today, more visitors than any other place in downtown Portland. *See p 9, bullet ①.*

The Pearl District & Old Town

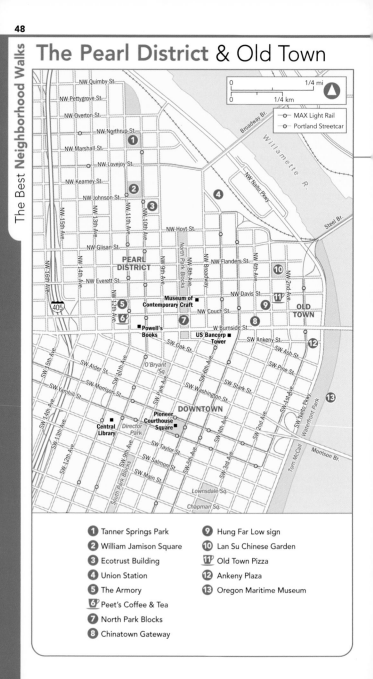

1 Tanner Springs Park
2 William Jamison Square
3 Ecotrust Building
4 Union Station
5 The Armory
6 Peet's Coffee & Tea
7 North Park Blocks
8 Chinatown Gateway
9 Hung Far Low sign
10 Lan Su Chinese Garden
11 Old Town Pizza
12 Ankeny Plaza
13 Oregon Maritime Museum

Northwest of downtown, Portland neighborhoods run the gamut from the art galleries, eateries, and condos of the upscale Pearl district to the slightly more disheveled streets of Old Town and Chinatown. Once a grubby district of warehouses and light industry, "the Pearl" is a case study in urban revitalization at its best, while Old Town holds on to its history, at least architecturally. (By the way, "Couch" street is pronounced "cooch," not like the piece of furniture.) START: **Streetcar NW 10th and Marshall.**

① ★ **Tanner Springs Park.** A quiet haven of burbling water and reedy grasses, this park re-creates a pocket of Portland's original wetlands and the stream that ran through it. A short walking trail leads past benches along a creek, and the east edge has a striking art installation: a wave-like wall of rusted railroad tracks studded with blue glass. ⏱ *15 min. NW Marshall & 11th aves.*

② ★ kids **Jamison Square Park.** Just 2 blocks away is another water-centric park, this one focused on a large fountain designed to mimic a tidal pool, with water spilling over low steps into a shallow pool that periodically empties and

refills. Take a look at the contemporary totem poles on 10th Street, the red-granite statue of a brown bear, and the urbane little French-style bosque. The park is named for William Jamison, whose art gallery got the Pearl District revitalization going in the 1990s. ⏱ *15 min. NW Johnson & 10th aves.*

③ ★ **Ecotrust Building.** One of the greenest of Portland's green buildings, this 2001 building made of recycled materials is now home to a collection of sustainable businesses and a Patagonia store. Portions of the original 1895 warehouse still stand along NW 10th Avenue. *721 NW 9th Ave.*

Union Station with its signature clock tower.

❹ ★ **Union Station.** Portland's grand rail terminal, built in 1896, reflected the city's position at the western end of the only sea-level route through the Cascades. The Italian Renaissance–style building was renovated in 1996 after a century of use, and now serves train and intercity bus travelers. Luckily, it kept its signature 150-foot Romanesque clock tower, with the addition of a neon "Go By Train" sign. You can get a taste of the building's glory days inside at Amtrak's only first-class Metropolitan Lounge on the West Coast, as well as at **Wilfs,** 800 NW 6th Ave. (☎ 503/223-0070; www.wilfsrestaurant.com), which combines turn-of-the-century ambience with organic local produce and live jazz from Wednesday through Saturday night. ⏱ *30 min. 800 NW 6th Ave. at Irving St.* ☎ *503/273-4865.*

❺ **The Armory.** Yet another historic building saved from the wrecking ball and repurposed, this unmistakable brick fortress anchors the downtown "Brewery Blocks." Constructed in 1891 to house the Oregon National Guard, it hosted presidential speeches, symphony concerts, and many, many casks of beer over the next century. A 2006 renovation made it one of the greenest buildings in the country— we're talking LEED platinum status—and the new home of Portland Center Stage, the city's largest theater company. The striking building now holds the 600-seat **Gerding Theater,** a small **studio theater,** and a **cafe.** Step into the lobby to see the grand staircase cantilevered off the second-floor balcony and the enormous ceiling trusses that give it such a roomy feel. ⏱ *15 min. 128 NW 11th Ave. at Davis St.* ☎ *503/445-3700. www.pcs.org. Ticket prices and showtimes vary.*

Recharge at 🏷️ **Peet's Coffee & Tea,** a long-established West Coast brand that serves strong coffee, chai lattes, tea drinks, and pastries. *1114 NW Couch.* ☎ *971/244-0452. $.*

❼ ★ **kids North Park Blocks.** Disconnected from the South Park Blocks by West Burnside Street, the North Park Blocks have a more urban feel than their counterparts, even though they have just as many old trees lining their sidewalks. The playground and basketball court are both popular, as are various artworks. Look for the 12-foot bronze

Repurposed on Purpose

Saving grand old buildings and giving them fresh new life helps to preserve Portland's unique architectural character. The 511 Federal Building at 511 NW Broadway is a case in point. Completed in 1918, this enormous Classical Revival-style structure was first used as a federal post office. A century later it was completely repurposed and reopened in 2015 after a $32-million makeover as the new home of the Pacific Northwest College of Art (www.pnca.edu). Today the building is called the **Arlene and Harold Schnitzer Center for Art.** Step inside for a look at the ornate interior and new atrium and galleries.

elephant sculpture between Burnside and Couch streets, an oversize replica of a Shang Dynasty wine pitcher, given to the city by a Chinese foundry owner. William Wegman, known for his photos of Weimaraner dogs, designed the checkerboard granite tiles of the "Portland Dog Bowl" between Davis and Everett streets to mimic a linoleum kitchen floor. Think of the bronze water bowl as a canine version of the Benson bubbler fountains (p 47). ⏱ *30 min. NW Park Ave. from Ankeny St. to Glisan St. Open daily.*

❽ ★ Chinatown Gateway. This ornate arch, built in 1985, is an impressive monument to the long history of Portland's Chinese residents. Artisans from Taiwan put it together and installed the two lion statues on either side. (The one on the left, Yin, protects the young, and Yang, the one on the right, protects the country.) The 38-foot

Lion statues guard the Chinatown Gateway.

The serene Lan Su Chinese Garden.

White Stag Sign

One of Portland's most distinctive symbols greets drivers and cyclists crossing the Burnside Bridge into downtown: a bounding neon stag above the words "Portland Oregon," enclosed by an outline of the state. The wording has gone through more revisions than a breakup letter, starting in 1940 when it was built to advertise White Satin Sugar. The building's next tenant conveniently shared an adjective, so the sign read "White Stag Sportswear" until 1995, when it was changed to read "Made in Oregon," with "Old Town" the latest subtitle. The current arrangement went up in 2010. (If you're around during the holidays, notice how easily the stag is transformed into Rudolph the Red-Nosed Reindeer.)

The White Stag sign.

high structure is decorated with 78 dragons and 58 mythical characters, including the Chinese characters for "Portland Chinatown" on the south side and "Four Seas, One Family" on the north side. ① 5 min. NW 4th Ave. at Burnside St.

❾ ★ **Hung Far Low sign.** Chinatown's other landmark earns its share of giggles, but this pagoda-topped marquee advertised a real

restaurant here from 1928 to 2005. (Like many Chinese-owned businesses in Portland, it relocated to SE 82nd Ave.) The two-story, 2,000-pound neon sign was restored and–ahem–re-erected in 2010. ① 5 min. NW 4th Ave. at Couch St.

❿ ★★★ **Lan Su Chinese Garden.** Complete your Chinatown visit with a stop at this astonishingly authentic classical Chinese garden, occupying a full block on the neighborhood's eastern side. You'll feel like you've stepped off a boat in ancient Suzhou, the coastal Chinese city where the entire garden was designed, packed up, and exported to be reassembled here in 2001. In the lakeside Tower of Cosmic Reflections, the pagoda-style **Teahouse** (☎ 503/224-8455) offers a contemplative spot to watch the light change over the plantings and classical Chinese pavilions. *See p 17, bullet* ⑤.

At the distinctive ⑪ **Old Town Pizza,** a pizzeria housed in a former hotel, step up to the old reception desk to order a slice, and keep an eye out for Nina, the resident ghost. ⏱ *15 min. 226 NW Davis St.* ☎ *503/222-9999. $.*

⑫ ★ **Ankeny Plaza.** Once the city's nexus of business and entertainment, this triangular plaza in Old Town is now home to the popular **Portland Saturday Market** of craft vendors (see p 78). At the plaza's center you'll see the neoclassical bronze and granite **Skidmore Fountain,** the oldest piece of public art in the city. For the fountain's grand opening in 1888, local brewer Henry Weinhard offered to pump beer through it using firehoses. (For some reason, city leaders turned him down.) Many of the nearby buildings, built of brick and cast iron in the late 19th century, are part of the Skidmore/Old Town National Historic District. *SW 1st Ave. & SW Ankeny St.*

⑬ ★ kids **Oregon Maritime Museum.** After the steam-powered sternwheeler tug *Portland*—the last

A neoclassical bronze detail from the Skidmore Fountain.

of its kind to operate in the United States—was retired in 1981 after 3 decades of service, it was restored to house a collection of maritime artifacts, ship models, and other nautical memorabilia. Youngsters can putter around a children's corner with a working ship's whistle and other hands-on goodies. The ship itself is the real attraction, though, as you'll discover on a tour with one of the expert docents, who will lead you around from pilot house to engine room. ⏱ *30 min. On the Willamette River in Waterfront Park, at Pine St.* ☎ *503/224-7724. www.oregonmaritimemuseum. org. Open Wed, Fri–Sat 11am–4pm. Admission $7 adults, $5 seniors 62 and over and children 6–17.*

Northwest Portland

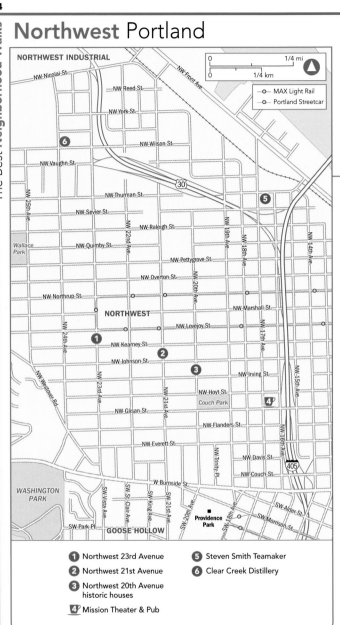

NORTHWEST INDUSTRIAL

NW Nicolai St

NW Reed St

NW York St

NW Wilson St

NW Front Ave

NW Vaughn St

⑥

NW Thurman St

NW Sevier St

NW Raleigh St

⑤

NW Quimby St

NW 22nd Ave

NW Pettygrove St

NW Overton St

NW 20th Ave

Wallace
Park

NW 25th Ave

NW Northrup St

NORTHWEST

NW Marshall St

NW 18th Ave

NW 19th Ave

NW 14th Ave

NW Lovejoy St

NW 17th Ave

NW 24th Ave

①

NW Kearney St

②

NW Johnson St

③

NW Irving St

NW 23rd Ave

NW 21st Ave

NW Hoyt St

Couch Park

④

NW Glisan St

NW Westover Rd

NW Flanders St

NW 15th Ave

NW Everett St

NW Trinity Pl

NW Davis St

405

NW Couch St

W Burnside St

WASHINGTON
PARK

SW Vista Ave

SW St. Clair Ave

SW King Ave

SW 21st Ave

SW 20th Ave

Providence
Park

SW 18th Ave

SW Alder St

SW Morrison St

SW Park Pl

GOOSE HOLLOW

0   1/4 mi
0   1/4 km

○— MAX Light Rail
○— Portland Streetcar

30

① Northwest 23rd Avenue
② Northwest 21st Avenue
③ Northwest 20th Avenue
   historic houses
④ Mission Theater & Pub
⑤ Steven Smith Teamaker
⑥ Clear Creek Distillery

Portland's northwest corner is a neighborhood of tree-shaded Victorian homes, postwar apartment buildings, and modern mansions overlooking downtown and the river. It's one of the city's wealthier districts, more compact than the flat eastside without feeling claustrophobic—on the contrary, with Arlington Heights and Forest Park rising to the west, it feels more like you're on the edge of a forest. On weekends and during the summer, visitors flock to the destination shopping and dining streets, NW 21st and NW 23rd avenues. It's easy to navigate, especially in the "Alphabet District" where the street names are ordered accordingly. START: **Bus: 15 or 77; Streetcar: NW 23rd & Marshall.**

NW 23rd Avenue shopping.

❶ ★★ **Northwest 23rd Avenue.** From West Burnside to Thurman Street, NW 23rd Avenue is an almost continuous string of restaurants, cafes, boutiques, coffee shops, and bars. Detractors may dismiss it as "trendy-third," but it's the commercial heart of this part of town, and definitely one of the destination shopping and dining stretches in Portland. There's a lovely residential area around NW 23rd and Lovejoy, where most of the Victorian- and Edwardian-era homes are located, called **Nob Hill** because it was built to rival San Francisco. The south end near

Burnside is home to large chain stores like Pottery Barn, Urban Outfitters, and Restoration Hardware. As you head north, you'll find more distinctive local places like **Gilt Jewelry** (720 NW 23rd Ave. at Johnson St.), **Two Tarts Bakery** (2309 NW Kearney St. at 23rd Ave.), and **Shogun's Gallery** (1111 NW 23rd Ave. at Marshall St.). Businesses peter out around Thurman Street, but take a left (west) for another 6 long blocks of options, plus, eventually, one of the main entrances to **Forest Park** (see p 86). ⏱ *1½ hr.*

The Lewis & Clark Exposition

Portland's population doubled between 1900 and 1910, a period of unprecedented growth not unlike what the city is experiencing today. That spurt of newbies was due, in large part, to the Lewis and Clark Exposition of 1905, a well-planned exercise in city boosterism that introduced tens of thousands of visitors to the city. The Exposition, which celebrated the 100th anniversary of Lewis and Clark's arrival, was a gigantic affair held on a site in Northwest Portland designed by John Olmsted, stepson of Frederick Law Olmsted, who designed New York's Central Park. In addition to gardens and pavilions, the Exposition featured a huge man-made lake and the world's largest log cabin, a Portland landmark until it burned down in the 1960s. Among other things, the Exposition spurred a new streetcar line and the creation of Oaks Park in Sellwood. Unfortunately, nothing remains of the Exposition site today: It's an industrial area next to the Vaughn Street exit of the I-5 freeway.

❷ ★ **Northwest 21st Avenue.** Two blocks east, NW 21st Avenue is similar to 23rd but leans more toward the food and drink side of things rather than upscale shopping. Take your pick from outstanding pastries at **Ken's Artisan Bakery** (338 NW 21st Ave. at Flanders), Italian and a chic bar at **Caffe Mingo** (807 NW 21st Ave. at Kearney St.), or French cooking at **Paley's Place** (1204 NW 21st Ave. at Northrup St.). The **Chop Butchery & Charcuterie** (735 NW 21st Ave. at Johnson St.) offers sandwiches and all things meat. The avenue is not all about eating, though; **Cinema 21** (616 NW 21st Ave. at Irving St.) shows independent and art-house movies. ⏱ *1½ hr.*

❸ ★ **Northwest 20th Avenue historic houses.** Gorgeous homes from the 1890s to the 1930s are everywhere up here, but you can find three excellent examples within a few blocks of Irving Street on 20th Avenue. (Keep in mind they're all private homes.) The 1892

Richardsonian Romanesque Revival at 615 NW 20th Ave. at Hoyt Street has the slate shingles, substantial stonework, and arched entrance porch that recall other examples of the style (Trinity Church in Boston, the American Museum of Natural History in New York City). The 1908 Colonial Revival at 733 NW 20th Ave. at Johnson Street was designed after a mid-18th-century Georgian colonial home in Pennsylvania, and the 1910 Craftsman at 811 NW 20th Ave. at Johnson Street is another example of the simple but handsome style. ⏱ *30 min.*

The singular 4️⃣ **Mission Theater & Pub** started as a Swedish Evangelical Mission in 1912, then served as a Longshoreman's Union hall before becoming Oregon's first theater-pub. Sit in the balcony or on the floor for recent movies, cult films, live music, or sporting events projected on a big screen. It's a McMenamins' joint, so, of course, pub fare, handcrafted ales, and wine are on sale. Thursday is pizza,

A spirits tasting at Clear Creek Distillery.

pint, and popcorn night for $10.
🕐 *1 hr. 1624 NW Glisan St. at
17th Ave.* ☎ *503/223-4527. www.
mcmenamins.com. Admission $4
adults, $3 children 11 and under.
Age 21 and over only, unless accom-
panied by parent. Event hours vary.*

⑤ ★ Steven Smith Teamaker.
The local founder of both Stash Tea
and Tazo Tea has launched his own
line of small-batch teas using rare,
high-quality ingredients. You can
come by the facility, an old black-
smith shop, to taste a cup or see the
teas being made and packaged. If
you're inspired, you can even blend
your own batch. 🕐 *30 min. 1626
NW Thurman St.,* ☎ *503/719-8752
or 800/624-9531. www.smithtea.com.*

*Open Mon–Fri 9am–5pm. Free
admission.*

⑥ ★ Clear Creek Distillery.
Traditional European brandy-making techniques meet northwest
Oregon's bounty of fruit at this artisan distillery, producer of fruit eaux
de vie, grappas, and wine brandies.
They only offer public tours around
Memorial Day and Thanksgiving,
but their tasting room and store are
open year-round. Come by to learn
about the process and sample spirits like their pear eaux de vie, with
the pear grown inside the bottle, or
their Islay-style Oregon single malt
whiskey. 🕐 *30 min. 2389 NW Wilson
St.* ☎ *503/248-9470. www.clear-
creekdistillery.com. Open Mon–Sat
9am–5pm. Free admission.*

A Swift September

Every evening in September, about an hour before sunset, hundreds of people congregate around Chapin Elementary School,
which sits in the middle of Wallace Park (west of NW 25th Ave. btw.
Pettygrove and Raleigh sts). They bring their own chairs or blankets
and camp out to watch a very special phenomenon: The Swift
Watch. Thousands of migrating Vaux's swifts circle in a vortex-like
cloud around the school's chimney, before flying in to roost for the
night. If you're a birder, or have kids, this is a sight worth planning
for. For information, go to **www.audubonportland.org**.

Northeast Portland

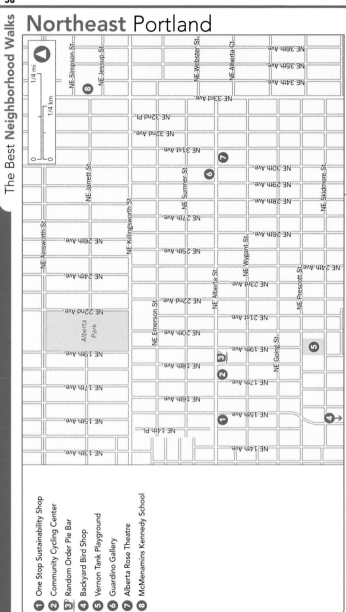

1 One Stop Sustainability Shop
2 Community Cycling Center
3 Random Order Pie Bar
4 Backyard Bird Shop
5 Vernon Tank Playground
6 Guardino Gallery
7 Alberta Rose Theatre
8 McMenamins Kennedy School

Northeast Portland is home to two of the oldest neighborhoods outside of the city center. Northeast Alberta Street between 12th and 33rd avenues—now known as the Alberta Arts District—has been "discovered" by young professionals looking for affordable real estate and a lively cultural mix, where Hispanic, Asian, and African-American businesses rub shoulders with hip cafes, boutiques, and trendy eateries. South of the Alberta Arts District, you may also want to stroll around the residential district known as Irvington, which lies between NE Fremont and NE Broadway streets. It's filled with a wonderful array of houses dating from the early 1900s to the late 1940s. At its western end is Grant Park, site of the Beverly Cleary Sculpture Garden (see p. 30). START: **Bus 8 or 72.**

❶ ★ **One Stop Sustainability Shop.** One of Portland's most common buzzwords, sustainability, is what this store is all about. Here you'll find everything from cleaning products to toys and pet beds that are nontoxic, fair-trade, recycled, and/or biodegradable, and often locally made. They offer classes on everything from candle-making and cooking to holiday crafts and wine-making. ⏲ *30 min. 1468 NE Alberta St.* ☎ *503/241-5404. www.growandmake.com. Open Tues–Fri 10am–6pm; Sat & Sun 10am–5pm.*

❷ ★ **Community Cycling Center.** Few places embody Portland's two-wheeled ethos as robustly as this nonprofit bike shop. They don't just fix and sell bikes, parts, and accessories—they also offer year-round programs that help get citizens up and rolling, including bike camps, bike clubs, maintenance classes, and bike drives for low-income families. ⏲ *15 min. 1700 NE Alberta St. at 17th Ave.* ☎ *503/287-8786. www.communitycyclingcenter.org. Open Tues–Sun 10am–6pm.*

The colorful mural of Community Cycling Center.

The Simpsons in Portland?

If some of the street names in Portland sound familiar, thank local son Matt Groening, creator of the TV hits *The Simpsons* and *Futurama*, who grew up in the Rose City.

In the Alphabet Historic District in Northwest Portland, look for (Mr.) Burns(ide), (Ned) Flanders, (Reverend) Lovejoy, and (Mayor) Quimby Streets. Mr. Burns's first name, Montgomery, also appears on a winding road in Southwest Portland, right by Washington Park.

Springfield has its own Springfield Gorge, which sounds an awful lot like the Columbia River Gorge. The Murderhorn, Springfield's highest peak, echoes Mount Hood.

And that benighted nuclear power plant where Homer Simpson works? That may have been based on the Trojan Nuclear Power Plant in Rainier, 46 miles north of Portland, which was decommissioned after 16 years due to safety and seismic concerns.

D'oh!

Refuel at **3** **Random Order Pie Bar** with a cup of java and a slice of homemade pie, either sweet or savory. Brandied peach and salted caramel apple are both specialties, and the Catalan vegetable potpie is enough for a meal. *1800 NE Alberta St. at 18th Ave.* ☎ *971/340-6995. www.randomordercoffee.com. Open Mon 6:30am–8pm; Tues–Sun 6:30am–11pm.* $.

4 ★ **kids** **Backyard Bird Shop.** Birding is big in Portland, so if you have any interest in our winged wonders, head over to this shop. It's not fancy, but it carries just about everything you need to nurture the birds in your backyard. There are feeders of every size, shape, and description, plus bulk birdseed mixes, birdhouses, birdbaths, and more. *1419 NE Fremont.* ☎ *503/455-2699. www.backyard birdshop.com. Open Mon–Sat 10am–6pm, Sun 10am–5pm.*

5 ★ **kids** **Vernon Tank Playground.** This small park and playground sits in the shadow of two huge cylindrical water tanks that look like something out of *War of the Worlds*. It's an odd mix, but it works; if the kids get tired of the swings and slides, you can play escape-the-invaders-from-outer-space instead. ⏱ *30 min. NE 21st Ave. & Prescott St. Open 5am–10pm.*

The restaurant at the remodeled Kennedy School, now a hotel.

6 ★ Guardino Gallery. Of all the galleries on Alberta Street, Guardino has the most reliably exciting mix of works and styles. From bronze sculptures and acrylic paintings to prints made with rusted car parts on old silk, there's always something unexpectedly intriguing on display. In the same building, you'll find the **HiiH Gallery,** selling handmade paper lamps; **Redbird Studio,** with handmade cards, stationery, clothes, and crafts; and **Suzette,** a creperie. ⏱ *1 hr. 2939 NE Alberta St. at 29th Ave.* ☎ *503/281-9048. www.guardinogallery.com. Open Tues 11am–5pm; Wed–Sat 11am–6pm; Sun 11am–4pm.*

7 ★ Alberta Rose Theatre. Yet another lovingly resurrected old theater, the 300-seat Alberta Rose started as a motion picture house in 1927, operated until 1978, and then sat dark for over 20 years. Now, however, it's a cultural fixture of the Albert Arts District, having been reborn as a space for independent films, comedy, acoustic music, and other live performances. During the show, they also serve regional libations and handmade Australian-style pies and other snacks. If you can, catch one of the regular tapings of *Live Wire! Radio,* a modern take on multi-performer vaudeville shows. ⏱ *2 hr. 3000 NE Alberta St. at 30th Ave.* ☎ *503/719-6055. www.albertarosetheatre.com. Showtimes vary, and some performances are 21 and over only.*

8 ★★ McMenamins Kennedy School. Detention never sounded as appealing as it does at this 1912 grade school, renovated and reopened in 1997 as a combination hotel, restaurant, and movie theater. There are no less than five bars on the premises, including the Detention Bar, Honors Bar, and the Boiler Room, all serving beer and other alcoholic tipples from the on-site brewery. Thirty-five guest rooms fill former classrooms, and the walls are covered in original art and historical photos. Relax in the hot outdoor soaking pool or catch a matinee on a couch in the second-run movie theater. For more on the Mecmenamins' family of hotels, theater, and pubs, see p. 137. *5736 NE 33rd Ave.* ☎ *503/249-3983. www.mcmenamins.com.*

Portland's Oldest Rose Garden

Visitors come from around the world to view the roses at the International Rose Test Garden in Washington Park (see p. 13). But Portland's first and oldest public rose garden, on the east side of town, is well worth visiting, too. **Peninsula Park Rose Garden** (700 N. Rosa parks Way; ☎ 503/823-3620; www.portlandonline.com/parks) still looks much as it did when it opened in 1913. Planted with over 7,000 roses, Oregon's only sunken rose garden features a lovely fountain and the city's sole remaining bandshell. One of Portland's best-kept secrets, the rose garden is at its fragrant and photogenic best in June.

Southeast Portland:
Hawthorne & Belmont

1. Belmont District
2. Avalon Theater
3. Historic Belmont Firehouse
4. Tao of Tea
5. Central Hawthorne District
6. Bagdad Theater & Pub
7. Fat Straw
8. Mike's Movie Memorabilia Collection
9. Laurelhurst Park

The giant sunflower painted at the intersection of SE 33rd Avenue and Yamhill Street captures the friendly, community-minded spirit of this part of town, where downtown can seem a world away, even though it's just a 5-minute drive across the river. The vibe here is mostly laid-back and unpretentious (Hawthorne was the hippie haunt of Portland back in the 1960s and '70s), with tree-lined streets and sometimes as much bicycle traffic as cars and trucks. START: Bus 14 or 15.

❶ ★ **Belmont District.** The commercial district on Southeast Belmont Street packs a lot into just a few blocks. You'll find shopping at eclectic places like **Noun** (3300 SE Belmont St. at 33rd Ave.), a quirky housewares/antiques store, and **Palace** (828 SE 34th Ave. at Belmont St.), with upscale new and vintage clothing for men and

women. Hungry? Grab a great burger at **Dick's Kitchen** (3312 SE Belmont St. at 33rd Ave.) and dessert at **Saint Cupcake,** which shares a storefront with Noun. Thirsty? **Stumptown Coffee Roasters** (3356 SE Belmont St. at 33rd Ave.) offers great people-watching, plus free coffee cuppings (aka tastings) daily at noon and 2pm in their Annex

Quirky antiques and housewares at Noun on Belmont Street.

two doors down. For nightlife, try the Avalon Theater (see below) or head downstairs to **The Liquor Store** (3341 SE Belmont St. at 33rd Ave.) for jazz and blues. *⏱ 1 hr. SE Belmont St. from 33rd to 35th aves.*

② ★ **kids Avalon Theater.** Second-run movies and nickel arcade games—is there any better way to stretch your date dollars? Oregon's oldest theater was also the first in the state with more than one screen. Now it shows films on three screens and fills the rest of the space with skee-ball, air hockey, and video games. You can even redeem your skee-ball tickets for prizes and candy. *⏱ 1 hr. 3451 SE Belmont St. at 34th Ave. ☎ 503/238-1617. Sun–Fri noon–midnight; Sat 11am–midnight. Movies are $3 for adults, $2.50 for seniors and children 11 and under. Arcade admission $2.90 adults, $2.40 children. Games are 20¢.*

③ ★ **kids Historic Belmont Firehouse.** Kids and history buffs love this 1912 firehouse, now home to a safety learning center and museum to Portland's firefighting history. Restored antique gear and equipment, like an 1859 Jeffers Sidestroke Handpump Fire Engine, are on display and, often, touchable. There's even a fire pole to

slide down! *⏱ 45 min. 900 SE 35th Ave. at 34th Ave. ☎ 503/823-3615. www.jeffmorrisfoundation.org. Open the 2nd Sat of every month, except July, Aug, and Dec, 10am–3pm, or by appointment.*

Coffee is definitely Portland's caffeine of choice, but tea has become increasingly popular. One of the best spots for a freshly brewed cup of organic assam or 0olong is the **④** **Tao of Tea.** The teahouse also offers a nice selection of simple, vegetarian-friendly snacks and meals. *3430 SE Belmont St. ☎ 503/736-0119. www.taooftea.com. $.*

⑤ ★ **Central Hawthorne District.** It's hard to beat Hawthorne Boulevard from 34th to 39th avenues for strollable shopping, eating, and entertainment. The whole commercial stretch runs roughly from 30th to 50th avenues, with everything from brewpubs to vintage clothing stores. The heart of it is in the high 30s, especially the block between 36th and 37th avenues, where you'll find the historic **Bagdad Theater & Pub** (see below), a branch of **Powell's Books** (3723 SE Hawthorne Blvd. at 36th Ave.) specializing in home and garden titles, and **Pastaworks** (3735 SE Hawthorne Blvd. at 36th Ave.), a European-style grocery and deli with an on-site eatery called **Evoe**. Other spots worth a stop are **Presents of Mind** (3633 SE Hawthorne Blvd. at 36th Ave.) for all things gift-oriented, **Imelda's Shoes and Louie's Shoes for Men** (3426 SE Hawthorne Blvd. at 34th Ave.), and **The Perfume House** (3328 SE Hawthorne Blvd.) for an outstanding selection of perfumes. ⏱ 2 hr. SE Hawthorne Blvd. btw. 34th & 39th aves.

⑥ ★ kids Bagdad Theater & Pub. One of Portland's grandest old theaters, veteran of some 25,000 shows over the decades, is now the main anchor of the Hawthorne commercial district. You can see a movie or show inside, knock back a tipple at one of two bars (including one behind the screen), or enjoy a meal and craft-brewed beer at the restaurant, which spills out onto the sidewalk in good weather. The building itself is eye-popping inside, restored to the full opulence of its inauguration in 1927, minus the spouting fountain. *See bullet ⑨, p 42.*

The name **⑦ Fat Straw** will make sense when you order your first glass of "boba" (bubble tea), an addictive milky Asian concoction with tapioca balls on the bottom. The less adventurous can go with fresh avocado or coconut-mango smoothies, or regular tea or coffee, and for noshing they serve tasty bánh mì (Vietnamese sandwiches). *4258 SE Hawthorne Blvd. at 42nd Ave. ☎ 503/233-3369. www.fat strawpdx.com. $.*

⑧ ★ Mike's Movie Memorabilia Collection. Ever wonder what happened to the knife from the shower scene in Hitchcock's *Psycho* or the monster costume from *Young Frankenstein*? They're here, inside the Movie Madness video store, along with other one-of-a-kind cinematic costumes and props. *See bullet ⑩, p 36.*

Imelda's Shoes on Hawthorne Boulevard.

Entertainment of all kinds at the Bagdad Theater & Pub.

⑨ ★ kids **Laurelhurst Park.**
Sometimes all you need at the end of a good walk is a shady patch of grass, maybe with a playground for the kids or a duck pond nearby. Look no further—Laurelhurst Park has all these and more, including a picnic grove, a hillside of rhododendrons, and trees that wouldn't be out of place on the slopes of Mt. Hood. Designed by the Olmsted Brothers (sons of the man responsible for New York's Central Park), in 2001 Laurelhurst became the first Portland city park to be listed on the National Register of Historic Places. There's an off-leash area for dogs and, across Stark Street, a children's playground next to tennis and basketball courts. (Originally, girls were supposed to play on the north side and boys on the south.) *See p 23, bullet* ⑦.

Feeding the ducks in Laurelhurst Park.

Inner Southeast

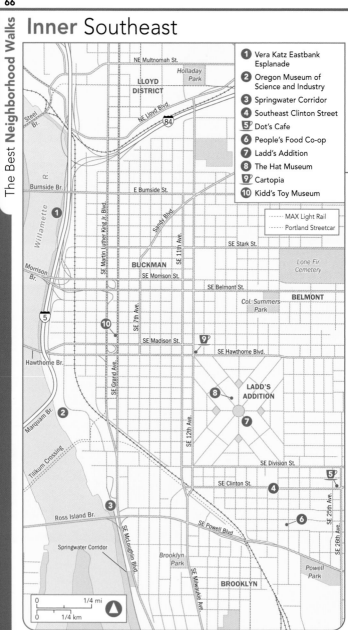

1. Vera Katz Eastbank Esplanade
2. Oregon Museum of Science and Industry
3. Springwater Corridor
4. Southeast Clinton Street
5. Dot's Cafe
6. People's Food Co-op
7. Ladd's Addition
8. The Hat Museum
9. Cartopia
10. Kidd's Toy Museum

----- MAX Light Rail
······ Portland Streetcar

NE Multnomah St.

Holladay Park

LLOYD DISTRICT

NE Lloyd Blvd.

84

Steel Br.

Willamette R.

Burnside Br.

E Burnside St.

SE Martin Luther King Jr. Blvd.

Sandy Blvd.

SE 11th Ave.

SE Stark St.

Lone Fir Cemetery

Morrison Br.

5

BUCKMAN

SE Morrison St.

SE Belmont St.

BELMONT

Col. Summers Park

SE 7th Ave.

SE Madison St.

10

Hawthorne Br.

SE Grand Ave.

9

SE Hawthorne Blvd.

2

LADD'S ADDITION

8

7

SE 12th Ave.

Marquam Br.

Tilikum Crossing

SE Division St.

5

SE Clinton St.

4

SE 25th Ave.

3

Ross Island Br.

SE McLoughlin Blvd.

SE Powell Blvd.

6

SE 26th Ave.

Springwater Corridor

Brooklyn Park

SE Milwaukie Ave.

Powell Park

BROOKLYN

0   1/4 mi
0   1/4 km

Portland's inner Southeast district starts with industrial warehouses near the river, but these soon give way to the mostly residential Hosford-Abernethy neighborhood. Cooperative gardens, alternative schools, and chicken coops are the norm around here, and you'll see more bicycles and baby strollers on the streets than cars. Small commercial hubs along Clinton and Division streets combine restaurants, coffee shops, and unique local businesses like Langlitz Leathers (2443 SE Division St.), creators of the first custom leather motorcycle jacket in 1947, and nearby Loprinzi's Gym (2414 SE 41st Ave.), an ultra-old-school bodybuilding facility. START: Bus 4, 6, 10, 14, 15, 31, 32, or 33.

1 ★★ kids **Vera Katz Eastbank Esplanade.** Start on the east bank of the Willamette, where this paved path runs for 1½ miles from the Hawthorne Bridge to the Steel Bridge, with great river-level views of the city's downtown skyline. Along the trail you'll pass public art, map markers, and interpretive panels on the history of the river and the area. A 1,200-foot floating walkway, the longest of its kind in the country, leads under the Burnside Bridge and past a public boat dock. (If you have time, the entire 2-mile loop across the Steel and Hawthorne bridges and through Governor Tom McCall Waterfront Park is a Portland must-do.) The esplanade is named for German-born Vera Katz, who was the first woman to serve as the Speaker of the Oregon House of Representatives and was mayor of Portland from 1993 to 2005. ⏱ 30 min.

2 ★ kids **Oregon Museum of Science and Industry.** At the southern end of the esplanade, "OMSI" boasts all the science-themed learning options you could ask for, from the hands-on exhibits, planetarium, and IMAX theater inside to an actual submarine moored in the river. This end of the

Joggers and cyclists on the Eastbank Esplanade's floating walkway.

Eastbank Esplanade, under the Marquam Bridge that carries I-5, is particularly pretty on sunny days, with views of the Hawthorne Bridge and the South Waterfront. ⏱ *1 hr. See p 18, bullet* ⑧.

❸ ★ **Springwater Corridor.** From OMSI, it's just a few blocks to the start of this 21-mile multiuse recreation trail that leads south and east through Sellwood to the town of Boring (seriously), part of a 40-mile paved loop that circles the entire city. It's worth exploring even just the beginning of the trail, which follows old trolley train tracks along the surprisingly green and quiet riverbank. *Note:* The restored Linneman Trolley Station near Southeast Powell and 185th is a convenient trailhead at which to park your car, fill your water bottles, or use the public restrooms. Another handy Springwater pit stop is at Southeast 136th, where a small market serves up liquid refreshment to thirsty trail warriors. ⏱ *30 min.*

❹ ★ **Southeast Clinton Street.** The stretch of Clinton Street from 16th to 26th avenues definitely takes the prize for cutest street ramble in this part of town.

It's dotted with local shops, cafes, bars, and restaurants, like the Swedish favorite **Bröder** (2508 SE Clinton St. at 25th Ave.; ☎ 503/736-3333), all without sacrificing its offbeat residential neighborhood vibe. The art-house **Clinton Street Theater** (2522 SE Clinton St. at 26th Ave.; ☎ 503/238-8899) has been showing the cult classic *The Rocky Horror Picture Show* every Saturday night since 1978, the longest run in the world. Beer lovers can even grab a pint at the tiny attached brewpub and bring it in with them. ⏱ *1 hr.*

One of Portland's best-loved dives, ❺ **Dot's Kitchen** is famous for its authentically awful '60s decor of velvet paintings and Naugahyde-covered booths. Aesthetics aside, it's also a place where you can relax with a snack or light meal. *2521 SE Clinton St.* ☎ *503/235-0203.*

❻ ★ **People's Food Co-op.** To experience Portland's fresh-local-seasonal-organic foodie mania in its purest essence—you know, the one behind all those "Know Your

Hands-on chemistry at OMSI.

Farmer" bumper stickers—pop into this cooperative grocery store just south of Clinton Street. Whether it's local dairy products in glass bottles or hard-to-find bulk items like mulberries and jungle peanuts, they have it, along with prepackaged snack items, a fresh juice cart, and a year-round farmers' market out front every Wednesday. ⏱ *15 min. 3029 SE 21st Ave.* ☎ *503/674-2642. www.peoples.coop. Daily 8am–10pm.*

7 ★ Ladd's Addition. North of the Clinton neighborhood is one of the city's most distinctive residential districts, a diagonal grid extending from Division to Hawthorne streets and 12th to 20th avenues. The highlights for visitors, aside from the general serenity of the place, are the five rose gardens incorporated into its layout. A large central garden and four smaller diamond-shaped ones at the points of the compass are all meticulously tended, with more than 3,000 plants representing over 60 varieties. ⏱ *45 min. See p 22, bullet* **5**.

8 ★ The Hat Museum. Tucked away in the Ladd-Reingold House, one of Ladd's Addition's older homes, is this incredible collection of chapeaus, a private labor of love that's one of the largest of its kind in the country. Some 1,300 hats date back to 1845 and include hats worn in the movies *Gangs of New York* and *Chicago*. A pre-arranged tour is required. ⏱ *1½ hr. See p 36, bullet* **9**.

The food cart "pod" at SE Hawthorne Street and 12th Avenue aka **9 Cartopia,** was one of the first to really take hold in Portland, and now has covered outdoor seating and an ATM. Take your pick from a vegan apple pie at **Whiffies Fried Pies** (☎ 503/946-6544), a freshly made wood-oven pizza at **Pyro Pizza** (☎ 503/929-1404), Belgian-style fries or poutine (fries with cheese curds and gravy) at **Potato Champion** (☎ 503/505-7086), or whichever of the other cart options strikes your fancy. *Hours vary, most carts open until 3am. $*

10 ★ Kidd's Toy Museum. The last stop on this tour is another private collection, this time of vintage games and toys. Owner Frank Kidd is full of stories about the items featured in this multi-room display, which includes an astonishing array of cast-iron mechanical banks and more than a few cringe-inducing examples from the less-PC days of yore. ⏱ *1 hr. See p 36, bullet* **8**.

Sellwood

1. Oaks Bottom Wildlife Refuge
2. Oaks Amusement Park
3. Sellwood Riverfront Park
4. Jade Bistro and Patisserie
5. Antique Row

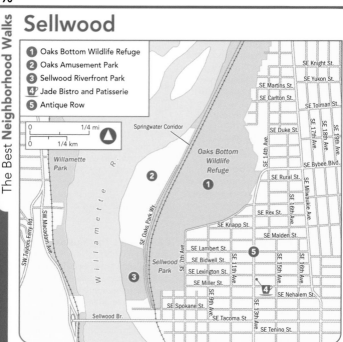

Although it is technically part of Portland, the Sellwood neighborhood feels more like a distinct village on the banks of the Willamette River, buffered as it is from the greater city by a long sweep of riverside parkland. You don't have to take a passenger ferry to get here, as folks did in the 19th century—you can even arrive by bike along the paved 4-mile-long Springwater Corridor trail south from OMSI (see p. 67). Most of Sellwood's boutiques, coffee shops, restaurants, and antiques stores are concentrated along SE Milwaukee Avenue and SE 13th Avenue. Otherwise, it's a homey neighborhood of bungalows and Victorian cottages, perfect for strolling, especially through the parks along the riverbank. START: **Bus 70.**

① ★ **Oaks Bottom Wildlife Refuge.** Two trails meander through this 141-acre flood-plain wetland on the east bank of the Willamette: a hiking trail along the river bluff, and the paved Springwater Corridor linking Sellwood and Portland's Eastbank Esplanade. The

woodlands, pond, and meadows are home to scores of birds, including quail, hawks, ducks, woodpeckers, and kestrels. You'll find plenty of great blue herons (Portland's official city bird), since this former construction landfill is close to the Ross Island rookery. If you forgot your field guide, just look up—the huge hand-painted mural on the outside of the Wilhelm Portland Memorial Mausoleum portrays many of the birds that call Oaks Bottom home, including a great blue heron and an osprey. This 43,000-square-foot mural is likely the largest of its kind in the country. 🕐 *45 min. Parking lots and trail heads at SE Milwaukee Ave. & McLoughlin Blvd., and at SE 7th Ave. & Sellwood Blvd.* ☎ *503/823-6131. Open daily 5am–midnight.*

② ★★ kids Oaks Amusement Park. It's hard to decide who enjoys this historic amusement park more: the tots riding the carousel and miniature train, the teenagers screaming themselves hoarse on the spinning modern rides, or the parents herding everyone around. Oaks is the oldest continually operating amusement park in the country, in business since 1905, and it

The Springwater Corridor links Sellwood to the Eastbank Esplanade.

Go-karting at the Oaks Amusement Park.

packs a lot into a little space on the bank of the Willamette, from the usual—carnival games, Ferris wheel, bumper cars—to the unique, including a 1912 carved carousel and large wooden roller-skating rink complete with pipe organ. *See p 30, bullet* **⑨**.

③ ★ Sellwood Riverfront Park. Just south of Oaks Bottom at the base of the old Sellwood Bridge (a new Sellwood Bridge has just replaced it), this riverside park offers hiking trails, picnic tables, beach access, and a small wetland reserve at its north end. The open grassy part includes an off-leash area for dogs. Walk north along the riverbank a little ways for a good view of downtown Portland, and to find a bobbing enclave of cozy houseboats. Free public concerts happen on Monday evenings in the summer. On the other side of SE Oaks Park Way (across the train tracks and Springwater Corridor), the larger **Sellwood Park** offers a swimming pool, sports fields and courts, and a playground. 🕐 *45 min. Entrance at SE Spokane St. & Oaks Pkwy. Open daily 5am–midnight.*

A Garden Paradise

If you're a garden lover, you'll find a rare botanical treasure in the Eastmoreland neighborhood about a mile northeast of Sellwood. At its peak from mid-March through early June, the **Crystal Springs Rhododendron Garden** (6015 SE 28th Ave.; ☎ 503/771-8386; www.rhodies.org) is home to more than 2,000 varieties of hybrid rhododendrons and azaleas. The palette of colors and array of delicious scents when the rhodies and azaleas are in flower will make your head swim. The 7-acre garden opened in 1956 on Shakespeare Island, where students at Reed College (right across the street) once staged the Bard's plays. With its lovely spring-fed lake (a favorite spot for birders), Crystal Springs served as the first test garden of the Portland chapter of the Oregon Rhododendron Society, established in 1950 and the first of its kind in the U.S.

A modern take on an Asian teahouse, **4** **Jade Bistro and Patisserie** offers a complete Vietnamese menu, but also a good selection of smaller bites such as baguette sandwiches, spicy green papaya salad, and, of course, lots and lots of teas. Desserts are a specialty, especially the Vietnamese Wedding Cake and chocolate-and-sea-salt French macaroons. *7912 SE 13th Ave., ☎ 503/477-8985. www.jadeportland.com $$.*

5 ★ **Antique Row.** If there's one thing Sellwood is known for, it's antiquing. More than 50 vintage stores along SE 13th Avenue brim with furniture, housewares, jewelry, and more. It may take some digging to find your own particular treasure, of course—but that's half the fun, right? Just a few outstanding examples include **Justin & Burks** (8301 SE 13th Ave. at Umatilla St.), the **Sellwood Collective Antiques** (8027 SE 13th Ave. at Spokane St.), and **Raven Antiques and Military** (7929 SE 13th Ave. at Miller St.). ⏱ *1 hr. Along SE 13th Ave., roughly btw. Malden & Tacoma sts.* ●

Shopping Best Bets

Best for **Books**
★★★ Powell's City of Books, *1005 W. Burnside St. (p 77)*

Best for **Shoes**
★★ Imelda's Shoes and Louie's Shoes for Men, *3426 SE Hawthorne Blvd. (p 80)*

Best for **Unexpected Discoveries**
★★ Cargo, *81 SE Yamhill St. (p 81)*

Best for **Toys**
★★★ Finnegan's Toys, *820 SW Washington St. (p 78)*

Best for **Vintage Surprises**
★★ Ampersand Vintage, *2916 NE Alberta St. Ste. B (p 77)*

Best for **Oregon Souvenirs**
★★ Made in Oregon, *Pioneer Place Mall (p 80)*

Best for **Hats**
★★ John Helmer Haberdasher, *969 SW Broadway Ave. (p 80)*

Best for **Kids' Clothes**
★★ Hanna Andersson, *327 NW 10th Ave. (p 78)*

Best for **Jewelry**
★★ Gilt, *720 NW 23rd Ave. (p 81)*

Best for **Sheer Selection**
★★ Pioneer Place, *700 SW 5th Ave. (p 82)*

Best for **Used Outfits**
★ Red Light Clothing Exchange, *3590 SE Hawthorne Blvd. (p 80)*

Best for **Records & CDs**
★★ Music Millennium, *3158 E. Burnside St. (p 82)*

Best for **Fragrances**
★ The Perfume House, *3328 SE Hawthorne Blvd. (p 78)*

Best to **Satisfy Your Inner Anime**
★★ Things From Another World, *2916 NE Broadway. (p 77)*; and ★★ Cosmic Monkey Comics, *5335 NE Sandy Blvd. (p 77)*

Best **Fresh, Local, Sustainable, Organic Produce Selection**
★★★ PSU Farmers Market, *SW Park Ave. at SW Montgomery St. (p 82)*

Previous page: Hand-painted flasks at Crafty Wonderland.

Downtown Shopping

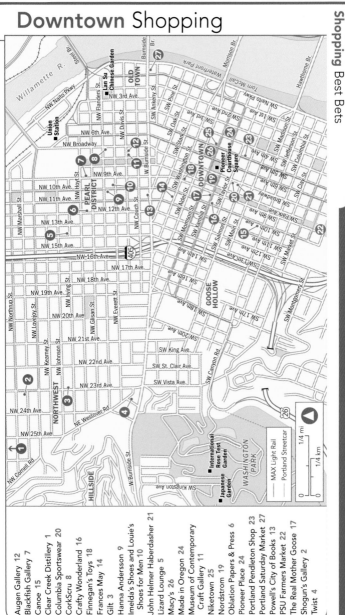

East Side Shopping

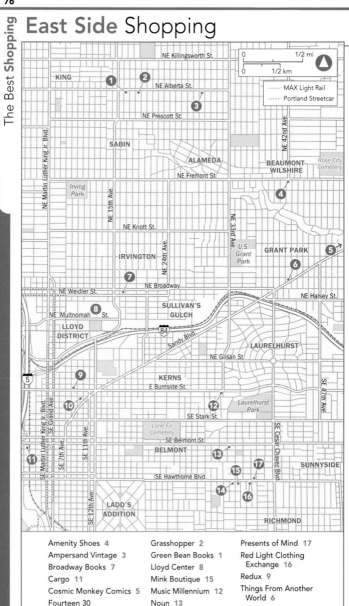

Amenity Shoes 4
Ampersand Vintage 3
Broadway Books 7
Cargo 11
Cosmic Monkey Comics 5
Fourteen 30 Contemporary 10

Grasshopper 2
Green Bean Books 1
Lloyd Center 8
Mink Boutique 15
Music Millennium 12
Noun 13
The Perfume House 14

Presents of Mind 17
Red Light Clothing Exchange 16
Redux 9
Things From Another World 6

Portland Shopping A to Z

Art

★★ Ampersand Vintage
ALBERTA   Are offbeat antique images your thing? Come here for 19th-century beetle prints, botanical cyanotypes, old mug shot photographs, and more. *2916 NE Alberta St. Ste. B (at 29th Ave.).* ☎ *503/805-5458. www.ampersand vintage.com. MC, V. Bus: 72. Map p 76.*

★ Augen Gallery DOWNTOWN
One of Portland's older galleries shows paintings and prints by regional artists and printmakers; their Pearl gallery (817 SW 2nd Ave.; ☎ 503/224-8182) specializes in prints. *716 NW Davis St. (at 7th Ave.).* ☎ *503/546-5056. www. augengallery.com. MC, V. Bus: 15 or 51. Map p 75.*

★★ Blackfish Gallery PEARL
This artist-owned cooperative isn't afraid to push the envelope, showing contemporary images as well as mixed-media pieces by lesser-known artists. *420 NW 9th Ave. (at Flanders St.).* ☎ *503/224-2634. www.blackfish.com. MC, V. Streetcar: NW 10th & Glisan; Bus: 17. Map p 75.*

★ Fourteen 30 Contemporary
SOUTHWEST   Step inside this immaculate white space to find works by artists on the cusp of breaking big. Often shows video and sculpture too, unusual for Portland. *1501 SW Market St.* ☎ *503/236-1430. www.fourteen30.com. MC, V. MAX: Goose Hollow/SW Jefferson St. Map p 76.*

Books, Magazines & Comics

★ Broadway Books NORTHEAST
At this quintessential neighborhood bookstore, the owners have an excellent eye for titles and are happy to point you to just the right book. *1714 NE Broadway Ave. (at 17th St.).* ☎ *503/284-1726. www. broadwaybooks.net. AE, MC, V. Bus: 9 or 77. Map p 76.*

★★ Cosmic Monkey Comics
NORTHEAST   No matter what you're after—anime, manga, graphic novels, or the latest titles—you'll find it here at Portland's premier comics store. Don't miss the back room, full of back issues and trades. *5335 NE Sandy Blvd. (at Sandycrest Terrace).* ☎ *503/517-9050. www.cosmicmonkeycomics.com. AE, MC, V. Bus: 12. Map p 76.*

★ Green Bean Books ALBERTA
Imagine the ideal children's bookstore: new and used books in a colorful space, comfy couches, and even a draping shady tree out back to read under. That's Green Bean Books. *1600 NE Alberta St. (at 16th Ave.).* ☎ *503/954-2354. www.green beanbookspdx.com. AE, MC, V. Bus: 72. Map p 76.*

★★★ Powell's City of Books
PEARL   What can you say about the world's best independent bookstore, a full city block of literature? Don't visit Portland without popping in at Powell's. *1005 W. Burnside St. (at 10th Ave.).* ☎ *503/228-4651. www.powells.com. AE, MC, V. Bus: 20; Streetcar: NW 10th & Couch. Map p 75.*

★★ Things From Another World
HOLLYWOOD   Fanboys rejoice! Not just wall-to-wall comics, but also collectible toys, figurines, games, and a couch for perusing. *2916 NE Broadway.* ☎ *503/284-2693. www.tfaw.com. MC, V. Bus: 17. Map p 76.*

The Best Shopping

Children's Clothing & Toys

★★★ Finnegan's Toys DOWNTOWN
This über-toystore is fun for adults, let alone kids, with an emphasis on learning and quality over buzzers and blinking lights. *820 SW Washington St.* ☎ *503/221-0306. www.finneganstoys.com. AE, MC, V. Streetcar: Central Library; MAX: Library/SW 9th Ave. Map p 75.*

★ Grasshopper ALBERTA
Handmade children's clothes, European toys, and award-winning books—this place is enough to make you want kids if you don't have them already. *1816 NE Alberta St. (at 18th Ave.).* ☎ *503/335-3131. www.grasshopperstore.com. MC, V. Bus: 72. Map p 76.*

★★ Hanna Andersson
PEARL   Children's clothes get a sunny Swedish makeover. This place is like catnip to grandparents, but the kids love it too. And there's a cupcake shop down the block! *327 NW 10th Ave. (at Flanders St.).* ☎ *503/321-5275. www.hannaandersson.com. AE, MC, V. Streetcar: NW 11th & Everett; Bus: 17. Map p 75.*

Cosmetics & Perfumes

★ The Perfume House HAWTHORNE
Everyone needs his or her own scent, right? Owner Chris Tsefalas, one of only 26 official "Noses" in the world, will help you discover your own special fragrance. *3328 SE Hawthorne Blvd. (at 33rd Ave.).* ☎ *503/234-5375. www.theperfumehouse.com. MC, V. Bus: 14. Map p 76.*

Crafts

★ Crafty Wonderland DOWNTOWN
What started as a temporary "pop-up shop" is now a permanent home to works by more than 90 talented local artisans, purveying cards, clothing, soap, pins, and much, much more. *802 SW 10th Ave. (at Yamhill St.).* ☎ *503/224-9097. www.craftywonderland.com. MC, V. Streetcar: Central Library. Map p 75.*

★ Museum of Contemporary Craft Gallery PEARL
The small retail gallery of this venerable museum sells jewelry and works made of ceramic, glass, fiber, metal, and wood, with prices toward the high end. *724 NW Davis St. (at 8th Ave.).* ☎ *503/223-2654. www.museumofcontemporarycraft.org. MC, V. Bus: 9 or 17. Map p 75.*

★ Portland Saturday Market OLD TOWN
Every Saturday and Sunday from March through December, some 300 craftspeople and artisans set up shop outdoors under the west end of the Burnside Bridge. Food and free entertainment round out the fun. *W. Burnside Ave. btw. SW 1st Ave. & SW Naito Pkwy.* ☎ *503/222-6072. www.portlandsaturdaymarket.com. MAX:*

Local artists are featured at Crafty Wonderland.

Powell's City of Books.

Skidmore Fountain; Bus: 16. Map p 75.

★ The Real Mother Goose

DOWNTOWN   If "unique" is your favorite shopping adjective, come to Portland's top crafts shop for one-of-a-kind jewelry, carved wood, blown glass, textiles, and accessories. *901 SW Yamhill St. ☎ 503/223-9510. www.therealmothergoose.com. (Also at Portland International Airport, Main Terminal; ☎ 503/284-9929). AE, MC, V. MAX: Library/SW 9th Ave. Map p 75.*

★ Twist NORTHWEST   True to

its name, this boutique gallery carries creative housewares and handmade jewelry, and everything is just a little bit out of the ordinary—in a good way. *30 NW 23rd Place (at Westover Rd.). ☎ 503/224-0334. www.twistonline.com. (Also at Pioneer Place Shopping Center, 700 SW 5th Ave.; ☎ 503/222-3137). AE, MC, V. Bus: 15 or 18. Map p 75.*

Department Stores

★ **Macy's** DOWNTOWN   The first six floors of the historic Meier & Frank building near Pioneer Courthouse Square are stuffed with clothes, accessories, housewares, makeup, and more. *621 SW 5th Ave. ☎ 503/223-0512. www.macys. com. (Also at 1001 Lloyd Center; ☎ 503/281-4797). AE, MC, V. MAX: Pioneer Courthouse/SW 6th Ave.; Bus: 1, 8, 12, or 94. Map p 75.*

★★ Nordstrom DOWNTOWN

Another national department store on Pioneer Square, Nordstrom offers a more intimate experience than Macy's and is famed for its shoe departments. For deals, try nearby **Nordstrom Rack** (245 SW Morrison St.). *701 SW Broadway Ave. (at Morrison St.). ☎ 503/224-6666. www.nordstrom.com. (Also at 1001 Lloyd Center; ☎ 503/287-2444). AE, MC, V. MAX: Pioneer Square. Map p 75.*

Fashion

★ Amenity Shoes NORTHEAST

Chic shoes (for both sexes) and bags in the Beaumont-Wilshire neighborhood. Many unique styles. *3430 NE 41st Ave. (at Fremont St.). ☎ 503/282-4555. www.amenity shoes.com. MC, V. Bus: 24 or 75. Map p 76.*

★ Frances May DOWNTOWN

Quite possibly the city's top women's boutique, with high-end brands befitting New York or Los Angeles. *1003 SW Washington St. (at 10th Ave.).* ☎ *503/227-3402. www.francesmay.com. AE, MC, V. Streetcar: SW 10th & Stark; Bus: 15 or 51. Map p 75.*

★★ Imelda's Shoes and Louie's Shoes for Men HAWTHORNE

Boots, high heels, Mary Janes: If they're stylish and go on your feet, they have 'em here, even though you might have to save up. *3426 SE Hawthorne Blvd.* ☎ *503/ 233-7476. www.imeldasandlouies. com. MC, V. Bus: 14. Map p 75.*

★★ John Helmer Haberdasher DOWNTOWN

Hankering for a hat? Craving a chapeau? John Helmer has been selling everything from fezzes to fedoras since 1921. *969 SW Broadway Ave. (at Salmon St.).* ☎ *503/223-4976. www.john helmer.com. MC, V. Bus: 15 or 51. Map p 75.*

★ Lizard Lounge PEARL

Hip duds for men and women, including sustainable local brand Nau and national ones like Billabong and Ray-Ban. And a ping-pong table. *1323 NW Irving St. (at 14th Ave.).* ☎ *503/416-7476. www.lizard loungepdx.com. MC, V. Bus: 17. Map p 75.*

★ Mink Boutique HAWTHORNE

Adorable dresses, sassy skirts, and fit-like-a-glove jeans—plus a friendly, knowledgeable sales staff—make this a neighborhood favorite. *3418 SE Hawthorne Blvd. (at 34th Ave.).* ☎ *503/232-3500. www.shopmink.com. MC, V. Bus: 14. Map p 76.*

★ Portland Pendleton Shop

DOWNTOWN Outfit yourself against the damp chill with fine wool fashions from this Northwest institution, and grab one of their famous blankets for home. *900 SW 5th Ave. (at Taylor St.).* ☎ *503/242-0037.*

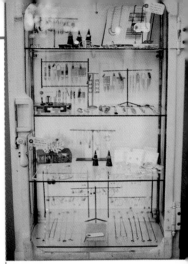

Artisan jewelry at Noun.

www.pendleton-usa.com. AE, MC, V. MAX: NW 6th & Davis sts.; Bus: 9 or 17. Map p 75.

★ Red Light Clothing Exchange

HAWTHORNE Vintage clothes are de rigueur to a certain stripe of Portlander, and this place has one of the biggest selections in town. *3590 SE Hawthorne Blvd. (at 36th Ave.).* ☎ *503/963-8888. www.red lightclothingexchange.com. MC, V. Bus: 14. Map p 76.*

Gifts & Souvenirs

★★ Made in Oregon DOWNTOWN

The full bounty of the Beaver State in one place—Tillamook cheese, Pendleton blankets, Timbers jerseys, Willamette pinots—make this the go-to place for local gifts. *Pioneer Place Mall, 340 SW Morrison St.* ☎ *503/241-3630. Also in the airport (*☎ *503/ 282-7827); and in Lloyd Center Mall, 1017 Lloyd Center (*☎ *503/282-7636). www.madeinoregon.com. AE, MC, V. MAX: Morrison/SW 3rd Ave. Map p 75.*

★ Presents of Mind HAWTHORNE

Locally made jewelry,

witty cards, and offbeat gifts make this an all-in-one gift-shopping destination. *3633 SE Hawthorne Blvd. (at 36th Ave.).* ☎ *503/230-7740. www.presentsofmind.tv. AE, MC, V. Bus: 14. Map p 76.*

Housewares

★★ **Canoe** DOWNTOWN   This modern home store is dedicated to good contemporary design and is great for thoughtful gifts, from kitchen items to home furnishings. *1233 SW 12th Ave.* ☎ *503/889-8545. www.canoeonline.net. AE, MC, V. Streetcar: SW 11th & Alder; Bus: 15 or 51. Map p 75.*

★★ **Cargo** SOUTHEAST   You'll feel like you've stumbled into a Chinese warehouse during a festival at this kaleidoscopic place, full of furniture, Asian antiques, paper lanterns, jewelry, and other sundries. *81 SE Yamhill St.* ☎ *503/209-8349. www.cargoinc.com. MC, V. Streetcar: SE M L King & Morrison; Bus: 6. Map p 75.*

★★ **Noun** BELMONT   Cleverly subtitled "A Person's Place for Things," this east-side nook carries charming antiques, artisan jewelry, and handmade stationery—plus

you enter through a cupcake shop. *3300 SE Belmont St. (at 33rd Ave.).* ☎ *503/235-0078. www.shopnoun. com. MC, V. Bus: 15. Map p 76.*

★ **Shogun's Gallery** NORTH-WEST   All things Asian, including Chinese and Japanese furniture, ceramics, bronze lanterns, and prints. *1111 NW 23rd Ave. (at Marshall St.).* ☎ *503/224-0328. www. shogunsgallery.com. MC, V. Streetcar: NW 23rd & Marshall; Bus: 15. Map p 75.*

Jewelry & Accessories

★★ **Gilt** NORTHWEST   A perennial favorite for its vintage and locally designed jewelry, including many one-of-a-kind items. It's hard to leave empty-handed. *720 NW 23rd Ave. (at Johnson St.).* ☎ *503/ 226-0629. www.giltjewelry.com. AE, MC, V. Bus: 15. Map p 75.*

★★ **Redux** SOUTHEAST   Everything in here used to be something else—all the wallets, belt buckles, ties, and jewelry are made of repurposed materials, often to charming and creative effect. *811 E. Burnside St. #110.* ☎ *503/231-7336. www. reduxpdx.com. MC, V. Bus: 12, 19, or 20. Map p 76.*

The vast stock at Imelda's shoes.

Downtown's fashionable Pioneer Place Mall.

Malls & Markets

★ **Lloyd Center** NORTHEAST
The biggest and oldest shopping
mall in the state is undergoing
some much-needed updating, but
it does have 200 stores, a multiplex
movie theater, and even a famous
indoor ice rink. *Btw. NE Multnomah
& NE Halsey sts., from 9th to 13th
aves.* ☎ *503/282-2511. www.lloyd
center.com. MAX: Lloyd Center/NE
11th Ave.; Bus: 8, 9, 70, 73, or 77.
Map p 76.*

★★ **Pioneer Place** DOWN-
TOWN   The most fashionable
shopping center in downtown, Pioneer Place has everything from an
Apple Store to Victoria's Secret,
plus a Regal cinema and a food
court. *700 SW 5th Ave. (at Morrison
St.).* ☎ *503/228-5800. www.pioneer
place.com. MAX: Mall/SW 4th Ave.;
Bus: 1, 8, 12, or 94. Map p 75.*

★★★ **PSU Farmers Market**
DOWNTOWN   The biggest and
by far most popular of Portland's six
seasonal open-air markets, the one
at PSU fills 2 full park blocks with
fresh-off-the-farm produce, flowers,
cheese, wine, meat, seafood, and
other goodies. *SW Park Ave. at SW
Montgomery St.* ☎ *503/241-0032.
www.portlandfarmersmarket.org.*
*Free admission. Streetcar: SW Park &
Mill. Map p 75.*

Music/CDs

★★ **Music Millennium** LAUREL-
HURST   Think of it as the musical
equivalent of Powell's Books: a vast
library of new and used, some rare
treasures, plus in-store performances
by top artists. *3158 E. Burnside St. (at
32nd Ave.).* ☎ *503/231-8926. www.
musicmillennium.com. MC, V. Bus:
20. Map p 76.*

Sportswear

★ **Columbia Sportswear**
DOWNTOWN   This local sportswear giant's flagship store brims with
rugged but tasteful gear designed
to last. Prices are lower at the factory outlet in Sellwood (1323 SE
Tacoma St.; ☎ 503/238-0118). *911
SW Broadway Ave. (at Taylor St.).*
☎ *503/226-6800. www.columbia.
com. AE, MC, V. MAX: Library/SW
9th Ave.; Bus: 15 or 51. Map p 75.*

★ **Niketown** DOWNTOWN   A
temple to athletic performance
(and the clothing thereof); fitting,
because Nike got its start here. The
outlet (2650 NE Martin Luther King
Jr. Blvd.; ☎ 503/281-5901) has
deals on last year's lines. *638 SW*

5th Ave. ☎ 503/221-6453. www.
nike.com. AE, MC, V. MAX: Pioneer
Sq. Map p 75.

Stationery & Cards
★ Oblation Papers & Press
PEARL Unique, high-quality stationery, cards, wedding invites, and
the like made on handmade paper
with century-old letterpresses. *516
NW 12th Ave. (at Hoyt St.).* ☎ *503/
223-1093. www.oblationpapers.com.
MC, V. Streetcar: NW 11th & Glisan.
Map p 75.*

Wines & Spirits
Clear Creek Distillery NORTH-
WEST Combine European
brandy-making techniques with
Oregon fruit and you get unbeatable eaux de vie, grappa, wine
brandy, and fruit liqueurs, all of
which you can sample here. *2389
NW Wilson St. (at 24th Ave.).*
☎ *503/248-9470. www.clearcreek
distillery.com. MC, V. Bus: 15, 17, or
77. Map p 75.*

CorkScru PEARL These guys
know their vintages, especially

Pear eau de vie at Clear Creek Distillery.

sub-$12 values, and they specialize
in wine six-packs from Italy, France,
and, of course, Oregon. *339 NW
Broadway (at Flanders St.).* ☎ *503/
226-9463. www.corkscru.biz. MC, V.
Bus: 9, 17. Map p 75.*

Lucinda Williams performs in-store at Music Millennium.

Farmers Markets

The Portland metro area supports no fewer than seven seasonal open-air farmers markets (**www.portlandfarmersmarket.org**). Along with farm-fresh produce and meats, you'll often find food carts, live music, crafts, and more.

- **Pioneer Courthouse Square Market:** SW Broadway & SW Morrison Street, Mondays June–September 10am–2pm.
- **Shemanski Park Market:** SW Park Avenue at SW Salmon Street, Wednesdays May–October, 10am–2pm.
- **Northwest Market:** NW 19th Avenue at NW Everett Street, Thursdays June–September, 2–6pm.
- **Buckman Market:** SE Salmon Street at 20th Avenue, Thursdays May–September, 3–7pm.
- **Portland State University Market:** Saturdays March–December, 8:30am–2pm.
- **King Market:** NE 7th Avenue at NE Wygant Street, Sundays May–October, 10am–2pm.
- **Kenton Market:** N McClellan & N Denver Street, Fridays June–September, 3–7pm. ●

Produce shopping at the PSU Farmers Market.

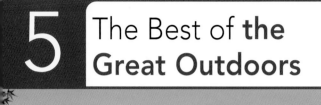

5 The Best of **the Great Outdoors**

Forest **Park**

0 — 1/4 mi	
0 — 1/4 km	

Leif Erikson Drive

Wild Cherry Trail

F O R E S T   P A R K

Wildwood Trail

NW Luzon St.

NW Industrial St.

NW St. Helens Rd.

NW 31st Ave.

NW 29th Ave.

NW Nicolai St.

NW 27th Ave.

NW Wilson St.   **NORTHWEST**
NW Vaughn St.

NW 32nd Ave.

NW Upshur St.
NW Thurman St.

3
4

NW Aspen Ave.

NW 53rd Dr.

Birch Trail

2

Holman Lane

Lower Macleay Trail

NW Cornell Rd.

Wildwood Trail

5

Macleay Park

NW Cumberland Rd.   **HILLSIDE**

1

NW Cornell Rd.

Upper Macleay Trail

Pittock Mansion

1 Audubon Nature Sanctuary
2 Wildwood Trail
3 Fat Tire Farm
4 The Clearing Café
5 Stone House

Extending 8 miles from the heart of Portland's West Hills, Forest Park points like a lush green finger toward the mouth of the Columbia River. At 5,100 acres, it's the U.S.'s largest natural forested area within city limits, with 8 square miles of fern-filled ravines, rushing streams, and towering firs, cedars, maples, and alders. The city's green playground is spiderwebbed with more than 80 miles of trails and fire lanes for hiking, biking, and running, and it is home to over 112 bird and 62 mammal species. There's no visitor center or main entrance; instead, at least 17 access points circle the park edge. (One main gateway is the start of Leif Erikson Drive, a 12-mile gravel road, at the end of NW Thurman St.) The west end of the park, away from downtown, is much wilder than the more heavily visited eastern end. START: **Drive to 5151 NW Cornell Rd.**

---

1 ★ kids **Audubon Nature Sanctuary.** Tucked up against Forest Park's southern side, this wildlife

rehabilitation center is home to all kinds of injured critters being nursed back to health (or simply

Previous page: Enjoying views of Mount Hood from the hilltop Pittock Mansion next to Washington Park.

Budding naturalists in Forest Park.

given a place to live), from coyotes to bald eagles. Sometimes they'll bring the animals out for up-close encounters. There's a gift shop and 150 acres of forest with a few miles of trails, including a newt-filled pond. It's also a good starting point for the Wildwood and Upper MacLeay trails in Forest Park proper. *See p 21, bullet* ❷.

❷ ★★ **Wildwood Trail.** Forest Park's longest trail is 27 sinuous miles of fern-lined curves, stream crossings, and switchbacks (plus another three in Washington Park). This National Recreation Trail is marked by blue diamonds and mile markers every quarter mile, which make it easy to take it in pieces; almost every loop hike in the park involves the Wildwood. Its eastern end sees a good bit of foot traffic, while its west end is in the wilder western part of the park.

❸ ★ **Fat Tire Farm.** Close to 30 miles of fire roads in Forest Park are open to mountain bikers. (Hiking trails, though, are not.) To try a few out, head to this bike shop 1 mile down Thurman Street from the Leif

Erickson Drive entrance, and rent a high-end mountain bike for the day. *2714 NW Thurman St. (at 27th Ave.).* ☎ *503/222-3276. www.fattirefarm. com. Bikes are $50–$200 for 24 hr. Mon–Fri 11am–7pm; Sat 10am–6pm; Sun noon–5pm.*

Fuel up for your hike (or recover afterward) with the healthy soups, panini, and tasty rice-and-bean bowls at ❹ **The Clearing Café** downhill from the Leif Erikson Drive entrance. *2772 NW Thurman St. (at 27th Ave.).* ☎ *503/841-6240. $.*

❺ ★ **Stone House.** This old restroom near Balch Creek, built by the Works Progress Administration in 1936, has grown evocatively moss-covered and roofless over the decades. It's a good place to take a break and ogle the park's largest tree: a 242-foot Douglas fir with a trunk 17½-feet in diameter. Reach it via the easy 1-mile Lower Macleay Trail from Lower Macleay Park (NW Upshur St. entrance).

Washington **Park**

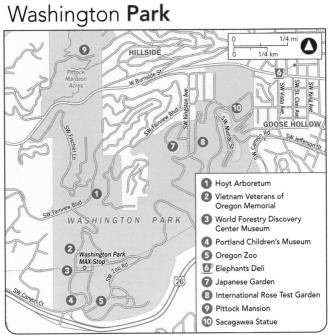

1. Hoyt Arboretum
2. Vietnam Veterans of Oregon Memorial
3. World Forestry Discovery Center Museum
4. Portland Children's Museum
5. Oregon Zoo
6. Elephants Deli
7. Japanese Garden
8. International Rose Test Garden
9. Pittock Mansion
10. Sacagawea Statue

Closer to downtown, Washington Park is Forest Park's more urbane neighbor, covering 410 acres of wooded hills between West Burnside Street and U.S. 26. It's basically an extension of the same steep forests that characterize Forest Park, but it offers visitors more developed attractions in a smaller space. Cougars don't roam the woods any more like they did in the 19th century, but plenty of dogs do, with their jogging owners in tow, on the park's 15-plus miles of trails. There's a Woodlands Trail, a Wildwood Trail, a Spruce Trail, a Hemlock Trail—well, you get the idea. A shuttle bus runs from the Washington Park MAX station (the deepest transit station in North America, at 260 ft. down) to the Japanese and rose gardens and the arboretum (daily June–Sept, and on weekends in May and Oct). START: **MAX Washington Park; Bus 63 on weekdays only.**

① ★★★ **Hoyt Arboretum.** This 187-acre reserve is much more than a woodsy park—it's a living museum of plants, with more than 8,000 shrubs and trees representing over 1,000 species from around the world, including dozens of species that are endangered in the wild. They're all thoughtfully organized according to where they came from and how they're related. There are always seasonal highlights, from the magnificent magnolias in the spring to fiery-colored maples in the fall and witch hazels in mid-winter. Twelve miles of hiking trails wind through the arboretum, including the Wildwood Trail that continues into Forest Park. At the visitor center, you can pick up maps for suggested routes of 1, 2, or 4 miles; 90-minute guided tours are offered on Saturdays at noon in the summer and fall. *Visitor Center: 4000 SW Fairview Blvd.* ☎ *503/865-8733. Free admission; guided tours $3 per person, most Sat June–Sept. Visitor center open Mon–Fri 9am–4pm; Sat–Sun 9am–3pm. Grounds open 6am–10pm daily. MAX: Washington Park. Bus: 63 on weekdays only.*

❷ ★ **Vietnam Veterans of Oregon Memorial.** On the south edge of the arboretum, this monument centers on a curved wall of black granite listing the names of

Strolling through Hoyt Arboretum.

Oregonians who died or went missing in action in Vietnam, echoing the more famous memorial in Washington, D.C. A spiral path leads past smaller walls with narratives from the conflict contrasted with local events. *4000 SW Canyon Rd. Open daily 5am–10pm. MAX: Washington Park. Bus: 63 on weekdays only.*

❸ ★ kids **World Forestry Discovery Center Museum.** The timber industry's major role in the development of the Pacific Northwest is the focus of this interactive museum geared mostly toward kids. Learn about the creatures that live under the forest floor, and ride into the (simulated) canopy of the Amazon rainforest. Out front sits "Peggy," a 33½-ton locomotive built in 1909, that hauled a billion feet of logs, more or less, in a 41-year career. *See p 22, bullet* ❸.

❹ ★★ kids **Portland Children's Museum.** Are the tykes tired of trees? The Children's Museum isn't huge, but it packs a lot into a modest space: a treehouse for story time, a studio for making art from recycled materials, a miniature grocery store complete with shopping carts and scanners. Kids 8 and under or so will love this place, often pleading for repeat visits to try it all. Traveling exhibits, classes, and visiting artists, musicians, and storytellers mean there's always something new on. *See p 27, bullet* ❷.

❺ ★★ kids **Oregon Zoo.** Completing the child-friendly trifecta at the southern end of Washington Park, Portland's zoo began in the 1880s with two bears—a grizzly named Grace and a brown bear named Brownie—and snowballed from there. Now it's the most popular paid attraction in the state, with 64 acres of felines, canines, primates, and pachyderms. Successful breeding programs for Asian elephants and California condors are the backbone of the zoo's conservation efforts. Two seasonal events pack in even more visitors: a summer evening open-air concert series and a winter holiday light show, best viewed from the ⅝-scale steam train that chugs as far as the Japanese and Rose Test gardens. *See p 15, bullet* ❶.

No relation to the zoo, the **Elephants Deli** just outside the park has wood-fired pizza, grilled sandwiches, and a sorely tempting dessert case. Try the garlic fries or a salad from the cold case. *115 NW 22nd Ave. (at Davis St.).* ☎ *503/299-6304. $$.*

❼ ★★★ **Portland Japanese Garden.** Near the top of Portland's must-see list is this tranquil oasis of gravel paths, koi ponds, pavilions, stone lanterns, and painstakingly manicured trees and shrubs. It's considered to be the most authentic Japanese garden outside of Japan. Plus, the views of Mount Hood from the Pavilion are outstanding. *See p 15, bullet* ❶.

❽ ★★★ **International Rose Test Garden.** Portland's floral showpiece was conceived in the chaos of World War I, when local rose hobbyists feared the bombs raining down on Europe might snuff out entire breeds. Today it's home to about 10,000 blooming bushes, with a focus on new hybrids. How pretty is this place? Put it this way: Every January 1st, even before the gardens open, there's already a line of couples outside applying for permits to have their weddings here. Kids may not be thrilled by rows upon rows of flowers, but just down SW Kingston Avenue is the **Rose Garden Children's Park,** a sprawling

Elephants at the Oregon Zoo.

Relaxing on the lawn outside the Pittock Mansion..

playground next to a picnic shelter in the zoo's old elephant barn. *See p 13, bullet* ⑩.

⑨ ★★ **Pittock Mansion.** While not technically in Washington Park, the mansion owned by Portland pioneer Henry Pittock is just across West Burnside Avenue (be careful crossing!) via the Wildwood Trail, and it's well worth a detour. Henry and his wife Georgiana, both first-generation Oregon immigrants, built this 23-room home in 1914 and lived in it until they died. Perched 1,000 feet above the city, the house incorporates English, French, and Turkish designs, but was built by Oregon craftsmen using Northwest materials. You can tour the interior or just enjoy the grounds, gardens, and views of Mt. Hood—first climbed by Pittock and four friends in 1854. *See p 12, bullet* ⑨.

⑩ ★ **Sacagawea Statue.** In the far northeast corner of the park, you'll find a relic of the Lewis & Clark Exposition held in 1905: a bronze sculpture of Sacagawea, the Shoshone woman who guided Lewis and Clark's expedition. Holding her baby Jean-Baptiste, she stands on a craggy boulder pointing to the horizon. Sculpted by Alice Cooper, the 7-foot-tall statue was the centerpiece of the expedition's main plaza; after the fair closed, the statue was moved here in 1906. It's located, appropriately enough, near the Lewis & Clark Memorial, a tall granite column erected in 1908. *SW Lewis & Clark Way. Open daily 5am–10pm. MAX: Washington Park. Bus: 63 on weekdays only.*

Portland **by Bike**

Map labels:

NW Glisan St.
Lan Su Chinese Garden ■
NW Everett St.
OLD TOWN
W Burnside St.
Burnside Br.
Steel Br.
SW Washington St.
SW Alder St.
Waterfront Park
Willamette R.
SE Martin Luther King Jr. Blvd.
SW Broadway
SW 2nd Ave.
SW Main St.
Morrison Br.
SW 4th Ave.
Tom McCall Waterfront Park
BUCKMAN
SE 7th Ave.
SW Naito Pkwy.
Hawthorne Br.
SE Madison St.
SE Hawthorne Blvd.
Oregon Museum of Science & Industry ■
SE Grand Ave.
SE 11th Ave.
LADD'S ADDITION
SE 12th Ave.
Marquam Br.
Tilikum Crossing
SE Division St.

1. Waterfront Bicycle Rentals
2. Travel Portland Visitor Information Center
3. Courier Coffee Bar
4. Tom McCall Waterfront Park
5. Hawthorne Bridge
6. Vera Katz Eastbank Esplanade
7. Springwater Corridor
8. Clinton Neighborhood
9. Tilikum Crossing Bridge
10. Hopworks BikeBar
11. Steel Bridge

0 ___ 1/2 mi
0 ___ 1/2 km

- - - MAX Light Rail
- - - Portland Streetcar

It's official: Portland is the most bike-crazy city in the country, with the highest percentage of cycling commuters (around 7%), some 315 miles of bikeways and bike lanes, and annual bike-related events like the 2-week Pedalpalooza every June. At last count the city boasted more than 30 artisan bike builders, a dozen bike clothing manufacturers, and some 75 bicycle sales/repair shops. This rolling tour offers a taste of what cycling in the City of Roses is all about. (*A word of caution:* Even though local motorists are used to driving around cyclists, and a surprising number of riders don't wear helmets, you should always wear one.) START: **MAX Oak/SW 1st Ave.; Bus 16.**

❶ ★ **Waterfront Bicycle Rentals.** Didn't bring your own wheels? Don't worry—they have you covered here, with hybrid city-ready bikes for rent, as well as kids' models, tandems, child trailers, and car bike racks. All rentals include a helmet, lock, map, and light. *10 SW Ash St. #100 (at Naito Pkwy.).*

☎ *503/227-1719. www.waterfront bikes.com. Daily 10am–6pm. Rentals $9/hr., $28/half-day, $40/24 hr., $100/week.*

❷ ★ **Travel Portland Visitor Information Center.** If you did bring your own bike, or if you just need a little more guidance (and a super-handy *Bike There!* map), head to Pioneer Courthouse Square for some in-person riding advice. Odds are, whoever's behind the counter got there on two wheels him- or herself that morning. *701 SW 6th Ave., Pioneer Courthouse Square.* ☎ *503/275-8355. www.travelportland.com. Mon–Fri 8:30am–5:30pm; Sat 10am–4pm; Sun May–Oct 10am–2pm.*

Time for some leg gasoline—sorry, caffeine—at this fittingly cycle-centric little coffee roaster and cafe, **3** **Courier Coffee Bar.** (They deliver their beans all over town—by bike, of course.) *923 SW Oak St.* ☎ *503/545-6444. $.*

4 ★★ **Governor Tom McCall Waterfront Park.** If you only ride one place in town, it should be through this skinny park along the Willamette, which makes a great start for longer rides as well. Stretching from the Steel Bridge almost to the Marquam (I-5) bridge, it passes fountains, cherry trees, the Saturday Market, and the 1947 stern-wheeler *Portland* (now home to the **Oregon Maritime Museum;** see p 53). It's also one segment of a popular 3-mile loop that crosses the Steel and Hawthorne bridges to the Eastbank Esplanade (see below). *See p 9, bullet* **2**.

5 ★★ **Hawthorne Bridge.** Cross the river on the country's oldest vertical-lift bridge, opened in 1910 and made bike-friendly in 1999 with wide sidewalks on both sides. Now it's Oregon's busiest bicycle bridge, with some 5,000 riders rolling across every day.

6 ★★ **kids** **Vera Katz Eastbank Esplanade.** Opened in 2001, this 1.5-mile bike and walking trail (named for former Mayor Vera Katz) links the Steel and Hawthorne bridges on the east bank of the Willamette. It crosses a 1,200-foot floating walkway under the Burnside Bridge and is one of the best places to see Portland's skyline in all its riparian glory. *See p 67, bullet* **1**.

7 ★ **kids** **Springwater Corridor.** Once a railroad that hauled passengers and produce, this 21-mile paved trail leads south from the Hawthorne Bridge and OMSI to the Sellwood neighborhood, home to Oaks Bottom Wildlife Refuge and Oaks Amusement Park. It's 4 miles to Sellwood, a scenic out-and-back ride along the river. From there, the trail turns east as part of the 40-mile loop around most of Portland (www.40mileloop.org). *See p 68, bullet* **3**.

8 ★ **Clinton Neighborhood.** After a detour down the

Let's Roll

If you'd like to explore more of the city, the Portland Bureau of Transportation offers free guided bike rides on Tuesday and Wednesday evenings at 6pm in the summer, arranged around themes such as public art and nature. The Tuesday rides start at Unthank Park (N. Failing St. at N. Commercial Ave.), and Wednesday rides start at Wellington Park (NE Mason St. at 67th Ave.). ☎ *503/823-5185; www.portlandonline.com/transportation.*

Cyclists on the bike-friendly Hawthorne Bridge.

Springwater Corridor and back, head east to this quintessential cycling neighborhood along SE Clinton Street and its popular bike path. There are dozens of places to eat, drink, and shop, concentrated around SE 21st and 26th avenues and at the "Seven Corners" intersection of SE Division Street and SE 20th Avenue. Look for the huge wheel of the penny-farthing outside **A Better Cycle** (2324 SE Division St.; ☎ 503/265-8595), a worker-owned bike shop. *See p 68, bullet* ❹.

⑨ ★ Tilikum Crossing Bridge. Returning west on Division Street, between SE 8th and SE 9th avenues across the train tracks you'll find SE Tilikum Way, leading to the new Tilikum Crossing Bridge, opened in 2015. It's the country's longest bridge dedicated exclusively to bikes, pedestrians, and public transportation (i.e., no cars allowed) and offers a great connection between the Central Eastside and OMSI over to the new high-rise South Waterfront District on the west side, with great city views

along the way. *South Waterfront OHSU Commons (west side) or SE Division St. (east side).*

Under the Tilikum Crossing bridge, follow the Eastbank Esplanade upriver to the Moda Center arena, where N. Interstate Avenue and then N. Williams Avenue take you to reach **⑩ Hopworks BikeBar,** the cycle-themed brewpub decorated with bike frames. Enjoy a giant pretzel and a pint from Hopworks Urban Brewery on the back patio—you earned it. *3947 N. Williams St. at Failing St.* ☎ *503/237-6258. $.*

⑪ ★ Steel Bridge. Return to the Eastbank Esplanade and complete your tour by crossing over the most eye-catching of Portland's bike-friendly bridges. Riders and pedestrians take a 220-foot cantilevered walkway suspended over the river, added on the south side in 2001. *See p 17, bullet* ❼. ●

Dining Best Bets

Menu shopping outside Ava Gene's.
Previous page: The namesake dish at Le Pigeon: grilled breast of pigeon.

Best **New Fine-Dining** Restaurant
★★★ Muselet $$$ *3730 SW Bond Ave. (p 105)*

Best for **Festive Celebrations**
★★★ Andina $$$ *1314 NW Glisan St. (p 100)*

Best for **Romance**
★ Chameleon $$$ *2000 NE 40th Ave. (p 102)*

Best for **Sophisticated Dining**
★★★ Blue Hour $$$ *250 NW 13th Ave. (p 101)*

Best **Dinner Entertainment**
★ Marrakesh $$ *1201 NW 21st Ave. (p 105)*

Best for **Gourmet Carnivores**
★★ Beast $$$ *5425 NE 30th Ave. (p 101)*

Best for **Vegetarians**
★ Prasad $ *925 NW Davis St. (p 107)*

Best **Italian**
★★ Caffè Mingo $$ *807 NW 21st Ave. (p 102)*

Best **Pan Asian**
★★ Pok Pok $$ *3226 SE Division St. (p 107)*

Best **Tapas**
★★★ Toro Bravo $$ *120 NE Russell St. (p 109)*

Best **Burger**
★★ Yakuza Lounge $$ *5411 NE 30th Ave. (p 110)*

Best **Pizza**
★ Apizza Scholls $$ *4741 SE Hawthorne Blvd. (p 100); and* ★ Ken's Artisan Pizza $$ *304 SE 28th Ave. (p 105)*

Best for **Deli Delights**
★ Kenny & Zuke's Delicatessen $$ *1038 SW Stark St. (p 105)*

Best **Cheap Eats**
★ Bunk Sandwiches $ *621 SE Morrison St. (p 102)*

Best **Brunch**
★★ Tasty n Alder $$ *580 SW 12th Ave. (p 108)*

Best **Happy Hour**
★ Saucebox $$ *214 SW Broadway Ave. (p 108)*

Best **Desserts**
★ Papa Haydn $$$ *701 NW 23rd Ave. (p 106)*

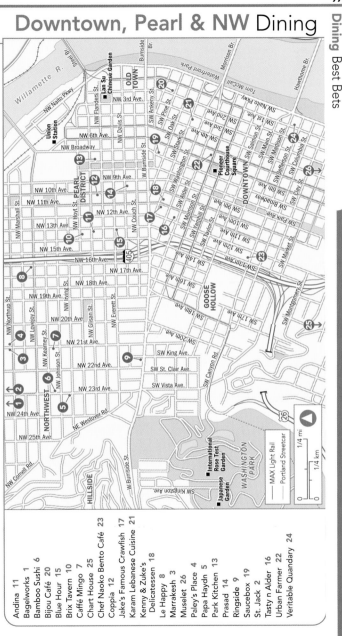

Andina 11
Bagelworks 1
Bamboo Sushi 6
Bijou Café 20
Blue Hour 15
Brix Tavern 10
Caffé Mingo 7
Chart House 25
Chef Naoko Bento Café 23
Coppia 12
Jake's Famous Crawfish 17
Karam Lebanese Cuisine 21
Kenny & Zuke's
  Delicatessen 18
Le Happy 8
Marrakesh 3
Muselet 26
Paley's Place 4
Papa Haydn 5
Park Kitchen 13
Prasad 14
Ringside 9
Saucebox 19
St. Jack 2
Tasty n Alder 16
Urban Farmer 22
Veritable Quandary 24

Southeast Dining

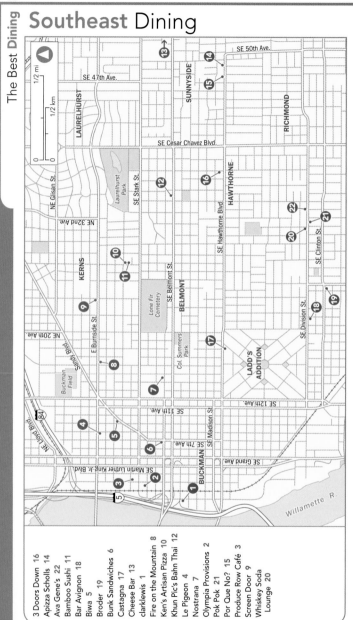

North & Northeast Dining

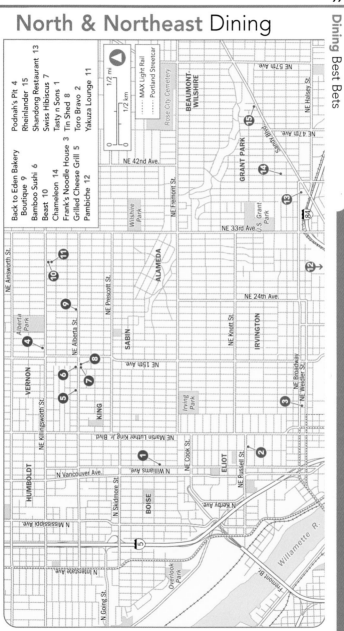

Back to Eden Bakery
Boutique 9
Bamboo Sushi 6
Beast 10
Chameleon 14
Frank's Noodle House 3
Grilled Cheese Grill 5
Pambiche 12

Podnah's Pit 4
Rheinlander 15
Shandong Restaurant 13
Swiss Hibiscus 7
Tasty n Sons 1
Tin Shed 8
Toro Bravo 2
Yakuza Lounge 11

1/2 mi
1/2 km

······ MAX Light Rail
······ Portland Streetcar

Dining A to Z

★ **3 Doors Down** HAWTHORNE *AMERICAN* This neighborhood cafe, hidden down a Hawthorne side street, is a local darling for its happy hour, attentive service, and overall bang for your buck. *1429 SE 37th Ave. (at Hawthorne Blvd.).* ☎ *503/236-6886. www.3doors downcafe.com. Entrees $18–$25. AE, MC, V. Dinner Tues–Sun. Bus: 14. Map p 98.*

★★★ **Andina** PEARL *PERUVIAN* You've never had *nuevo andino* cuisine like this: stuffed piquillo peppers, house-made ceviche, squash stew. Many plates are sized to share. Loud, lively atmosphere and very popular, so reserve in advance. *1314 NW Glisan St. (at 13th Ave.).* ☎ *503/228-9535. www.andina restaurant.com. Entrees $19–$30; small plates $9 and up. AE, MC, V. Lunch & dinner daily. Bus: 17. Map p 97.*

★ **Apizza Scholls** HAWTHORNE *PIZZA* Get in line early for some of Portland's best pizza—think hot truffle oil, goat horn peppers, and cured pork shoulder—and hope they don't run out of homemade dough, which does happen. *4741 SE Hawthorne Blvd. (at 48th Ave.).* ☎ *503/233-1286. www.apizza scholls.com. Pizzas $19–$25. AE, MC, V. Dinner daily, lunch Sat–Sun. Bus: 14. Map p 98.*

★★ **Ava Gene's** CLINTON *ITALIAN* The sophisticated, Italian-inspired cooking at this contemporary trattoria is inventive without being overly complicated. Share some smaller plates and split a pasta dish and you'll leave happy. *3377 SE Division. [tel]971/229-0571. www.avagenes.com. Entrees $18–$37. AE, MC, V. Dinner daily. Bus: 4. Map p 98.*

★ **Back to Eden Bakery Boutique** ALBERTA *BAKERY* This eco-conscious concern is your source for gluten-free vegan cookies, cakes, pies, and other goodies using mostly local, organic ingredients. Try a green tea whoopie pie. *2217 NE Alberta St. (at 23rd Ave.).* ☎ *503/477-5022. www.backtoeden bakery.com. Entrees $3–$8. MC, V. All meals daily. Bus: 72. Map p 99.*

★ kids **Bagelworks** NORTHWEST *BAGELS* Sometimes nothing will do but a toasted bagel with

Andina's sophisticated twist on Peruvian food.

Bar Avignon.

lox and cream cheese. That's when you head to Bagelworks, the bagel-centric sister of Kenny & Zuke's Delicatessen (p 105). Order a breakfast bagel sandwich or a big pastrami, turkey, or whitefish-filled bagel for lunch. *2376 NW Thurman St.* ☎ *503/954-1737. www.kennyand zukes.com/bagelworks. Entrees: $5–$17. AE, MC, V. Breakfast & lunch daily. Bus: 15. Map p 97.*

★ **Bamboo Sushi** LAURELHURST *SUSHI* The country's first certified sustainable sushi restaurant serves guilt-free seafood that happens to be delicious, too. Other locations: 836 NW 23rd Ave. (☎ 971/229-1925) and 1409 NE Alberta St. (☎ 503/889-0336). *310 SE 28th Ave. (at Pine St.).* ☎ *503/232-5255. www. bamboosushi.com. Entrees $9–$14; rolls $4–$8. AE, MC, V. Dinner daily. Bus: 20. Map p 97, 98, and 99.*

★ **Bar Avignon** CLINTON *PACIFIC NORTHWEST/FRENCH* Criminally delicious craft cocktails taste even better with foraged lettuces, homemade charcuterie, and artisan cheeses. Daily specials may range from rabbit agnolotti to halibut with onions. *2138 SE Division.* ☎ *503/517-0808. www.baravignon. com. Entrees $22–$27. MC, V. Dinner daily. Bus: 4. Map p 98.*

★★ **Beast** ALBERTA *FRENCH/ AMERICAN* Local celeb chef Naomi Pomeroy's meat-tastic prix-fixe meals—six-course dinners and a four-course brunch—will send vegetarians screaming, but make carnivores swoon. *5425 NE 30th Ave. (at Killingsworth St.).* ☎ *503/ 841-6968. www.beastpdx.com. AE, MC, V. Dinner Wed–Sat $102; Sun brunch $45. Bus: 72. Map p 99.*

★ **Bijou Café** DOWNTOWN *AMERICAN* Long before Portland had a food scene, Bijou was serving breakfast and lunch to happy downtown diners. It's the only place I know of that serves oyster hash. *132 SW Third Ave.* ☎ *503/222-3187. www.bijoucafepdx.com. Entrees $7–$15. AE, MC, V. Breakfast & lunch daily, dinner Friday. MAX: Oak St. Map p 97.*

★ **Biwa** INNER SOUTHEAST *JAPANESE* Come downstairs into this cozy space for Japanese comfort/bar food like ramen bowls, grilled rice balls, and pickled everything, plus loads of sake choices. *215 SE 9th St. (at Ash St.).* ☎ *503/239-8830. www.biwarestaurant.com. AE, MC, V. Dinner daily. Entrees $6–$13. Bus: 12, 19, 20, or 70. Map p 98.*

★★★ **Blue Hour** PEARL *MEDITERRANEAN/NEW AMERICAN* This long-established restaurant helped put Portland on the foodie map. The menu offers just a few choices, always deliciously prepared and beautifully served (try the 11-course tasting menu for $60). Expect only the freshest local ingredients and a superb wine list. A happy-hour hotspot for downtown and Pearl District professionals. *250 NW 13th St. (at Everett).* ☎ *503/226-3394. www.bluehour online.com. Entrees: $26–$38. AE, MC, V. Lunch & dinner Mon–Fri; dinner Sat. Bus: 17. Map p 97.*

★ **BRIX Tavern** PEARL *AMERICAN* This comfortable pub offers unpretentious but solid choices like wild-mushroom pizza, mac and cheese, and potpies, plus pool tables and sports on big screens. *1338 NW Hoyt St. (at 14th Ave.).* ☎ *503/943-5995. www.brixtavern. com. Entrees: $10–$24. AE, MC, V. Lunch & dinner Mon–Fri; all meals Sat & Sun. Bus: 17. Map p 97.*

★★ **Broder** CLINTON *SWEDISH Smaklig måltid!* Tuck into Danish pancakes, a Stockholm hot dog, and, of course, Swedish meatballs at this Scandinavian eatery. Their box lunch is a winner. **Broder Nord,** 2240 N. Interstate Ave. (☎ 503/282-5555) serves a smorgasbord dinner on Fridays. *2508 SE Clinton St. (at 25th Ave.).* ☎ *503/ 736-3333. www.broderpdx.com. Entrees: $7–$15. AE, MC, V. Breakfast & lunch daily. Bus: 10. Map p 98.*

★ **Bunk Sandwiches** INNER SOUTHEAST *SANDWICHES* Nationally known sandwiches? That's Bunk, an unprepossessing spot serving a delectable pork belly *Cubano* and roast chicken salad with applewood smoked bacon and avocado. Check the website for additional locations. *621 SE Morrison St. (at 6th Ave.).* ☎ *503/477-9515. www.bunksandwiches.com. Entrees $5–$11. MC, V. Breakfast &*

lunch Mon–Sat. Bus: 6 or 15. Map p 98.

★★ **Caffè Mingo** NORTHWEST *ITALIAN* If you're looking for a friendly neighborhood restaurant serving fine, simple Italian food made with exclusively local ingredients, show up at Mingo. But show up early or late, or you'll have to wait—they don't take reservations. *807 NW 21st Ave.* ☎ *503/226-4646. www.caffemingo.com. Entrees $12– $28. AE, MC, V. Dinner daily. Streetcar: NW 21st and Northrup. Map p 97.*

★★ **Castagna** HAWTHORNE *MODERN EUROPEAN* A prix-fixe dinner here is always a culinary adventure, with fresh ingredients and a mix of textures and flavors. (Cafe Castagna next door is less expensive and open for lunch.) *1752 SE Hawthorne Blvd. (at 17th Ave.).* ☎ *503/231-7373. www. castagnarestaurant.com. Prix-fixe dinner $65; chef's tasting menu $98. AE, MC, V. Dinner Wed–Sat. Bus: 14. Map p 98.*

★ **Chameleon** HOLLYWOOD *AMERICAN* This under-the-radar spot earns raves for its intimate atmosphere and covered patio as well as its butternut squash ravioli and coconut cream pie. Most of the veggies come from the chef's own farm. *2000 NE 40th Ave. (at U.S. Grant Place).* ☎ *503/460-2682. www.chameleonpdx.com. Entrees: $17–$24. AE, MC, V. Dinner Wed– Sat. Bus: 75. Map p 99.*

★ **Chart House** SOUTHWEST *SEAFOOD* Portlanders have patronized this restaurant for decades. Foodies tend to ignore it, because there's nothing cutting-edge about its traditionally prepared dishes. But for reliably good food with the best view over the city, drive up the hill to Chart House. *5700 SW Terwilliger Blvd.* ☎ *503/246-6963. www.chart-house.*

Portland Specialties

Regional Northwest cooking is distinguished by its pairings of meats and seafood with local greens, vegetables, fruits, and wines. Salmon (king, Coho, chinook) is the king of Oregon fish, though, to be honest, most of the salmon served and sold in Portland is now from Alaska. Salmon is prepared in seemingly endless ways, but the most traditional method is **alder-planked salmon.** This Native American cooking style entails preparing a salmon as a single filet, splaying it on alder wood, and slow-cooking it over a wood fire. After salmon, **Dungeness crab** is the region's top seafood offering, and crab cakes are ubiquitous on Oregon restaurant menus. The Northwest's combination of climate and abundant rainfall has also made Oregon one of the nation's major **fruit-growing regions,** producing a bounty of pears, blushing Rainier cherries, and berries, including strawberries, raspberries, and blackberries. **Wild mushrooms** are featured on menus throughout the city, so by all means try to have some while you're here. Oregon is also one of the few places in the world that still grows **hazelnuts.**

com. Entrees $23–$37. AE, MC, V. Lunch Sun–Fri, dinner daily. Bus: 1. Map p 97.

★ **Cheese Bar** BELMONT CHEESE/DELI Portlander Steve Jones won the 2011 Cheesemonger Invitational, making him the world's top cheese expert, so you know his upscale deli is the place for quality fromage. 6031 SE Belmont St. (at 61st Ave.). ☎ 503/222-6014. www.cheese-bar.com. Entrees $8–$11. Tues–Sun lunch & dinner. Bus: 15 or 71. Map p 98.

★ **Chef Naoko Bento Café** DOWNTOWN JAPANESE This downtown lunch favorite uses organic local ingredients in its noodle dishes, tofu bowls, and bento box lunches (try the wild Coho salmon). 1237 SW Jefferson St. (at 12th Ave.). ☎ 503/227-4136. www.chefnaoko.com. Entrees $8–$19. AE, MC, V. Lunch Tues–Sat, dinner Wed–Fri. Bus: 6, 43, 45, 55, 58, or 68. Map p 97.

★ **clarklewis** INNER SOUTHEAST AMERICAN Sliding garage doors and a fireplace give one of Portland's original farm-to-table restaurants a "cozy industrial" atmosphere, with an open kitchen turning out savory dishes such as grilled lamb and black cod. 1001 SE Water Ave. #160 (at Yamhill St.). ☎ 503/235-2294. www.clarklewispdx.com. Entrees $14–$39. AE, MC, V. Lunch Mon–Fri; dinner Mon–Sat. Bus: 15. Map p 98.

★ **Coppia** PEARL ITALIAN People come to this quiet wine bar in the Pearl for the golden beet soufflé and delicious Piedmontese specialties like risotto or pappardelle with oxtail ragu—or simply to enjoy a glass of wine with an appetizer. 417 NW 10th Ave. ☎ 503/295-9536, www.coppiapdx.com. SE, MC, V. Entrees $22–$28. Dinner Tues–Sat. Streetcar: NW 10th & Glisan. Map p. 97.

Wings and craft beer at Fire on the Mountain.

★ **Farm Café** INNER SOUTH-EAST *AMERICAN* This snug, homey place with creaky floors brings the farm to your table in the form of imaginative dishes like beet carpaccio, herb-crusted tofu, and a standout veggie burger. *10 SE 7th Ave. (at Burnside).* ☎ *503/736-3276. www.thefarmcafe.com. Entrees $16–$23. AE, MC, V. Dinner daily. Bus: 12, 19, or 20. Map p 98.*

★ **Fire on the Mountain** INNER SOUTHEAST *BBQ* Buffalo wings are raised to high art here, with sauces ranging from bourbon chipotle and Jamaican jerk to raspberry habanero and the tongue-melting "El Jefe." Great beer selection, too. Check website for additional locations. *1706 E. Burnside St. (at 17th Ave.).* ☎ *503/230-9464. www.portlandwings.com. Entrees $7–$12. MC, V. Lunch & dinner daily. Bus: 20. Map p 98.*

★ **Frank's Noodle House** LLOYD DISTRICT *KOREAN/CHINESE* Hand-pulled noodles made daily are the specialty here, but the dumplings and hot-and-sour soup are also worth writing home about. *822 NE Broadway St. (at 8th Ave.).* ☎ *503/288-1007. www.franksnoodlehouse portland.com. Entrees $6–$10. MC, V. Lunch & dinner Mon–Sat. Bus: 9. Map p 99.*

★ kids **Grilled Cheese Grill** ALBERTA *SANDWICHES* Set in an old school bus, the grill turns out all kinds of gourmet grilled cheese, from the "Kindergartner" to "The Cheesus," a hamburger between grilled-cheese sandwiches instead of a bun. They also have a cart downtown at SW Alder and Washington. *1027 NE Alberta Ave. (at 11th Ave.).* ☎ *503/206-8959. www.grilledcheesegrill.com. Entrees $4.50–$9. MC, V. Lunch Fri–Sat; lunch & dinner Sun–Thurs. Bus: 72. Map p 99.*

★ **Jake's Famous Crawfish** DOWNTOWN *SEAFOOD* Portland's oldest restaurant, this atmospheric warren of rooms features an ornate bar and a menu dedicated to fish and meat (come at happy hour for less expensive samplings). Jake's is famous for its crawfish, which come from Lake Billy Chinook in Oregon's high desert. *401 SW 12th Ave. (at Stark St.).* ☎ *503/226-1419. www.jakesfamouscrawfish.com. Entrees $15–$48. AE, MC, V. Street-car: SW 10th & Stark. Map p 97.*

★ **Karam Lebanese Cuisine** DOWNTOWN *LEBANESE* Friendly service and consistently good Lebanese dishes like cous-cous, kebobs, and fresh-baked pita bread set this place apart. *515 SW 4th Ave.* ☎ *503/223-0830. www.karamrestaurant.com. Entrees*

$14–$24. AE, MC, V. Lunch & dinner Mon–Sat; Sun 2pm–8pm. Bus: 15 or 51. Map p 97.

★ Kenny & Zuke's Delicatessen DOWNTOWN DELI
This is Portland, so it's not just deli food, it's *artisan-made* deli food. All your faves are here: chicken soup with matzah balls, chopped liver, latkes, blintzes, knishes, and overstuffed hot pastrami sandwiches. *1038 SW Stark St. (at 11th Ave.).* ☎ 503/222-3354. www.kennyandzukes.com. Entrees $10–$18. AE, MC, V. All meals daily. Streetcar: SW 10th & Stark. Map p 97.

★ Ken's Artisan Pizza SOUTHEAST PIZZA
With an emphasis on the "art," the crisp-crusted pies at this stone-oven pizzeria are worth the wait. Try the prosciutto and *soppressata. 304 SE 28th Ave. (at Pine St.).* ☎ 503/517-9951. www.kensartisan.com. Entrees $12–$17. AE, MC, V. Dinner daily. Bus: 28. Map p 98.

★ Khun Pic's Bahn Thai BELMONT THAI
It looks like someone's old Victorian house, but it's actually one of Portland's best and most authentic Thai eateries, albeit with leisurely service. *3429 SE Belmont St. (at 34th Ave.).* ☎ 503/235-1610. Entrees $8–$14. No credit cards. Dinner Tues–Sat. Bus: 15. Map p 98.

★ Le Happy NORTHWEST CREPERIE
Sweet and savory crepes are served in a charming red-walled nook that seems straight out of a Paris side street (disco ball notwithstanding). *1011 NW 16th Ave. (at Lovejoy St.).* ☎ 503/226-1258. www.lehappy.com. Entrees $7–$12. MC, V. Dinner Mon–Sat, brunch Sat–Sun. Streetcar: NW Lovejoy & 18th; Bus: 77. Map p 97.

★★★ Le Pigeon INNER SOUTHEAST FRENCH
An open kitchen and a James Beard Award–winning chef (Gabriel Rucker) make this snug spot a consistent standout. It's a creative spin on traditional French cuisine, from pigeon confit ramen to beef cheek bourguignon. Make a reservation now. *738 E Burnside St. (at 7th Ave.).* ☎ 503/546-8796. www.lepigeon.com. Entrees $23–$29. AE, MC, V. Dinner daily. Bus: 12, 19, or 20. Map p 98.

★ Marrakesh NORTHWEST MOROCCAN
Come for the live belly dancing and North African atmosphere; stay for the surprisingly good five-course dinners. *1201 NW 21st Ave. (at 22nd St.).* ☎ 503/248-9442. www.marrakeshportland.com. 5-course dinner $20. MC, V. Dinner daily. Streetcar: NW Northrup & 22nd; Bus: 77. Map p 97.

★★★ Muselet SOUTH WATERFRONT MODERN AMERICAN
Chef Greg Zanotti's creative cuisine draws out rich, mouthwatering flavor from local produce, meats, and fish, while Ron Acierto's encyclopedic wine knowledge takes flight with superlative, sometimes surprising wine pairings. Voted one of *Wine Spectator*'s top U.S. wine restaurants in 2015. *3730 SW Bond Ave.*

The open kitchen at Le Pigeon.

Spot prawns at Muselet.

☎ 503/265-8133. www.museletpdx. com. Entrees $23–$26. AE, MC, V. Dinner Tues–Sat. Streetcar: SW Lane & Bond. Map p 97.

★★ **Nostrana** INNER SOUTH-EAST *ITALIAN* The wood-oven pizzas and pork dishes get high praise, but it's the little things that make Nostrana special, such as the fresh-crushed olive oil and a great happy hour. *1401 SE Morrison St. (at 14th Ave.).* ☎ *503/234-2427. www. nostrana.com. Entrees $16–26. AE, MC, V. Lunch Mon–Fri; dinner daily. Bus: 15. Map p 98.*

★ **Olympia Provisions** INNER SOUTHEAST *CHARCUTERIE* The big lighted sign that says "MEAT" sums up this place, with some of the best chorizo, pancetta, and charcuterie plates in town. There's now a second location at 1632 NW Thurman St. (☎ 503/894-8136). *107 SE Washington St. (at 2nd Ave.).* ☎ *503/954-3663. www.olympia provisions.com. Entrees $14–$18. AE, MC, V. Lunch & dinner daily. Bus: 6 or 15. Map p 98.*

★★ **Paley's Place** NORTHWEST *FRENCH Iron Chef America* winner Vitaly Paley turns out exquisite razor clams and rabbit ravioli in a Victorian home in Nob Hill. If it's nice out, sit on the front porch. *204 NW 21st Ave. (at Northrup St.).*

☎ *503/243-2403. www.paleysplace. net. Entrees $19–$39. AE, MC, V. Dinner daily. Streetcar: NW Northrup & 22nd; Bus: 17. Map p 97.*

★ **Pambiche** NORTHEAST *CUBAN* You can't miss the colorful building, and the Cuban creole food is just as exciting, from the "Plato Comunista" to the classic pork sandwiches. *2811 NE Glisan St. (at 28th Ave.).* ☎ *503/233-0511. www.pambiche.com. Entrees $11– $21. AE, MC, V. Breakfast Sat & Sun; lunch & dinner daily. Bus: 19. Map p 99.*

★ **Papa Haydn** NORTHWEST *AMERICAN* Sure, they serve fresh, tasty bistro fare here—they've been doing that for over 35 years—but what really packs 'em in is the dessert case, groaning with banana cream pies and chocolate hazelnut tortes. *701 NW 23rd Ave. (at Irving St.).* ☎ *503/228-7317. www.papa haydn.com. Entrees $13–$26. AE, MC, V. Lunch & dinner daily. Bus: 15. Map p 97.*

★ **Park Kitchen** PEARL *AMERICAN* This parkside place has an ever-changing menu of fresh, seasonal delights, both standard-size and small plates (hot and cold) to share. The blind tasting menu is always a hit. *422 NW 8th Ave. (at*

Glisan St.). ☎ 503/223-7275. www.
parkkitchen.com. Entrees $28–$36;
small plates $6–$14. MC, V. Dinner
daily. Bus: 17. Map p 97.

★ **Podnah's Pit** NORTHEAST
BBQ Don't mess with Texas—
BBQ, that is, done right at this
northeast staple. Pulled pork, ribs,
potato salad, it's all Lone Star–
worthy. *1625 NE Killingsworth St. (at
17th Ave.).* ☎ *503/281-3700. www.
podnahspit.com. Entrees $13–$17.
MC, V. Breakfast Sat & Sun; lunch &
dinner daily. Bus: 8. Map p 99.*

★★ **Pok Pok** SOUTHEAST
ASIAN You may not be able to
pronounce the dishes, but Pok
Pok's tasty take on Asian street
food makes it a local favorite. Their
Vietnamese fish-sauce wings are a
Portland classic. It's so good that
Pok Pok has now expanded to New
York and L.A. *3226 SE Division St. (at
32nd Ave.).* ☎ *503/232-1387. www.
pokpokpdx.com. Entrees $12–$17.
MC, V. Daily lunch & dinner. Bus: 4.
Map p 98.*

★ **Por Que No?** HAWTHORNE
MEXICAN "Why not?" indeed—
this colorful *taqueria* is *excelente* in
the atmosphere and food departments both, especially during
sidewalk-dining weather. *4635 SE

Hawthorne Blvd. (at 46th St.).* ☎ *503/
954-3138. www.porquenotacos.com.
Tacos $3–$4; entrees $6–$10. MC, V.
Daily lunch & dinner. Bus: 14. Map
p 98.*

★ **Prasad** PEARL *VEGETARIAN*
The name means "holy food" in
Sanskrit, and the menu is all
organic, gluten-free, and vegan.
Choices include curry bowls, wraps,
salads, and tempeh scrambles. *925
NW Davis St. (at 9th Ave.).* ☎ *503/
224-3993. www.prasadcuisine.com.
Entrees $6–$9. MC, V. All meals
daily. Streetcar: NW 10th & Everett.
Map p 97.*

★ **Produce Row Café** INNER
SOUTHEAST *AMERICAN* Gourmet pub fare—cheese steaks,
meatloaf, a stellar burger—and an
outdoor patio put this Inner Southeast destination on the map. Try a
beer and whiskey pairing. *204 SE
Oak St. (at 2nd Ave.).* ☎ *503/232-
8355. www.producerowcafe.com.
Entrees $9–$13. AE, MC, V. Lunch &
dinner daily. Bus: 6. Map p 98.*

★ **Rheinlander** NORTHEAST
GERMAN Sauerbraten, bratwurst,
and käsespätzle, with servers in
lederhosen and accordion music
while you eat—it's like a mini–Bavar-
ian village on NE Sandy. *5035 NE

Casual Prasad specializes in organic, vegan food.

Sandy Blvd. (at 50th Ave.). ☎ 503/288-5503. www.rheinlander.com. Entrees $13–$19. AE, MC, V. Dinner Tues–Sun. Bus: 12. Map p 99.

★★★ Ringside Steakhouse

NORTHWEST *STEAKHOUSE* Dining at Stumptown's oldest steakhouse isn't cheap, but the steaks are super, there's an outstanding wine list, and the onion rings were praised by James Beard himself. That's why this place has been popular for 70 years and is still going strong. 2165 W. Burnside St. (at King Ave.). ☎ 503/223-1513. www.ringsidesteakhouse.com. Entrees $30–$65. AE, MC, V. Dinner daily. Bus: 15, 18, or 20. Map p 97.

★ Saucebox

DOWNTOWN *PAN-ASIAN* A chic crowd sips creative cocktails and nibbles dim sum and curries as DJs spin in the evenings; earlier, smart singles come for the super happy hour deals. 214 SW Broadway (at Pine St.). ☎ 503/241-3393. www.saucebox.com. Entrees $15–$28. AE, MC, V. Dinner Tues–Sat. Bus: 1, 12, 19, 20, 54, or 56. Map p 97.

★ Screen Door

SOUTHEAST *SOUTHERN* Here you'll find favorites from across the South, including shrimp and grits, beef brisket, and their celebrated buttermilk-battered fried chicken. There's always a line out the door for brunch—for a reason. 2337 East Burnside St. (at 24th Ave.). ☎ 503/542-0880. www.screendoorrestaurant.com. Entrees $10–$18. MC, V. All means daily. Bus: 20. Map p 98.

★ Shandong Restaurant

NORTHEAST *CHINESE* A bright spot in Portland's subpar Chinese-food scene, Shandong offers reasonably priced dishes from northern China, such as crab curry and cherry pork, plus house-pulled noodles. 3724 NE Broadway St. (at 37th Ave.). ☎ 503/287-0331. www.

Dry aged beef at Ringside Steakhouse.

shandongportland.com. Entrees $8–$13. MC, V. Lunch & dinner daily. Bus: 77. Map p 99.

★ Swiss Hibiscus

ALBERTA *SWISS* Swiss cuisine with a Hawaiian influence (seriously), from fondue to Wiener schnitzel, draws fans to this hidden gem—as does the famous house-made dressing. 4950 NW 14th Ave. (at Alberta St.). ☎ 503/477-9224. www.martinsswissdressing.com. Entrees $9–$23. AE, MC, V. Lunch Sat; dinner Tues–Sat. Bus: 72. Map p 99.

★ St. Jack

NORTHWEST *FRENCH* Many of the dishes here are old-school classics, with tastes that are delightfully worth rediscovering. Try the cream of tomato soup cooked in a puff pastry, seared foie gras on brioche, or the Lyonnaise onion tart. 1610 NW 23rd Ave. ☎ 503/360-1281. www.stjackpdx.com. Entrees $11–$37. AE, MC, V. Dinner daily. Bus: 15. Map p 97.

★★ Tasty n Alder

DOWNTOWN *PACIFIC NORTHWEST* Bustling, unpretentious, and on everyone's short list, this downtown restaurant—sister to Toro Bravo and Tasty n Sons (below)—is a shared-plate kind of place with dishes like crispy fried oysters, radicchio salad, and alder-plank-baked salmon. Super-popular weekend brunch. *580 SW 12th Ave. (at Alder St.).* ☎ *503/621-9251. www.tastynalder.com. Entrees $15–$44. AE, MC, V. All meals daily. Streetcar: SW 11th & Alder. Map p 97.*

★★ Tasty n Sons NORTH PORTLAND *AMERICAN* Bacon-wrapped dates with maple syrup are just the beginning at this new American diner spot, a sister restaurant to Toro Bravo (below) and Tasty n Alder (above). Known for gourmet breakfasts. *3808 N. Williams Ave. (at Failing St.).* ☎ *503/621-1400. www.tastynsons.com. Entrees $8–$22. AE, MC, V. Lunch & dinner daily. Bus: 44. Map p 99.*

★ Tin Shed ALBERTA *AMERICAN* Vying for the title of top breakfast in town, this "garden cafe" also does a solid lunch and dinner—but starters like sweet-potato French toast and biscuits with bacon gravy are the real draw. *1438 NE Alberta St. (at 14th Place).* ☎ *503/288-6966. www.tinshedgardencafe.com. Entrees $7–$22. MC, V. All meals daily. Bus: 72. Map p 99.*

★★★ Toro Bravo NORTHEAST *SPANISH* The tapas at "Brave Bull" are so good you might choose to defend them from your friends instead of share. Standouts include duck liver mousse terrine and the salt cod fritters. *120 NE Russell St. (at Rodney Ave.).* ☎ *503/281-4464. www.torobravopdx.com. Entrees $7–$17. AE, MC, V. Dinner daily. Bus: 6. Map p 99.*

★ Urban Farmer DOWNTOWN *STEAKHOUSE* A dramatic position in the atrium of the Nines Hotel sets off mostly organic, farm-to-table fare, with outstanding cuts of beef. *525 SW Morrison St. (at 5th Ave.).* ☎ *503/222-4900. www.urbanfarmerrestaurant.com. Entrees $25–$60. AE, MC, V. All meals daily. MAX: Pioneer Courthouse/SW 6th Ave. Bus: 1, 8, 12, or 94. Map p 97.*

★ Veritable Quandary DOWNTOWN *AMERICAN* With a prime outdoor patio at one end of the Hawthorne Bridge, this 45-year-old institution is known for its *osso buco* and duck-confit spring rolls. *1220 SW 1st Ave. (at Jefferson St.).* ☎ *503/227-7342. www.veritablequandary.com. Entrees $13–$20. AE, MC, V. Lunch & dinner daily. Bus: 4, 6, 10, 14, 31, 32, 33, or 99. Map p 97.*

Spanish tapas rule at Toro Bravo.

Pod People

Food carts have become an official Portland "thing," on par with fixed-gear bikes and well-worn raingear. These mobile food purveyors merge the city's idiosyncratic, do-it-yourself vibe with the local passion for good food at a good price, and there are at least a few hundred on the streets at any given time. They usually park in one place for a while (check www.foodcartsportland.com for updates), forming "pods" (clusters) all over town. Here are some of the most established spots:

Downtown:
- SW 5th Avenue and Oak Street (the original Portland pod)
- SW 9th and 10th avenues between Alder and Washington streets

North & Northeast:
- N Mississippi Street and Skidmore Avenue (Mississippi Marketplace)
- NE 21st Avenue and Alberta Street

Southeast:
- SE 12th Avenue and Hawthorne Boulevard (Cartopia)
- SE 32nd Avenue and Division Street (D Street Noshery)
- SE 43rd Avenue and Belmont Street (Good Food Here)
- SE 50th Avenue and Ivon Street (A La Carts)

Downtown "pod" of food trucks.

★ **Whiskey Soda Lounge** DIVISION *THAI* Enjoy *ahaan kap klaem*, Thai drinking food, across the street from sister restaurant Pok Pok: dried cuttlefish, drinking vinegars, and, yes, those famous fish-sauce wings. *3131 SE Division St. (at 31st Ave.).* ☎ *503/232-0102. www. whiskeysodalounge.com. Entrees $5–$18. MC, V. Dinner daily. Bus: 4. Map p 98.*

★★ **Yakuza Lounge** NORTH-EAST *JAPANESE* Serving a contemporary version of Japanese bar food, this place offers many small plates to share and an outstanding burger (Kobe beef, of course). *5411 NE 30th Ave. (at Killingsworth St.).* ☎ *503/ 450-0893. www.yakuza lounge.com. Entrees $10–$18. AE, MC, V. Dinner Wed–Sun. Bus: 72. Map p 99.* ●

Portland Nightlife

0 _____ 1/2 mi
0 _____ 1/2 km

----- MAX Light Rail
----- Portland Streetcar

Previous page: A flaming cocktail at the Driftwood Room.

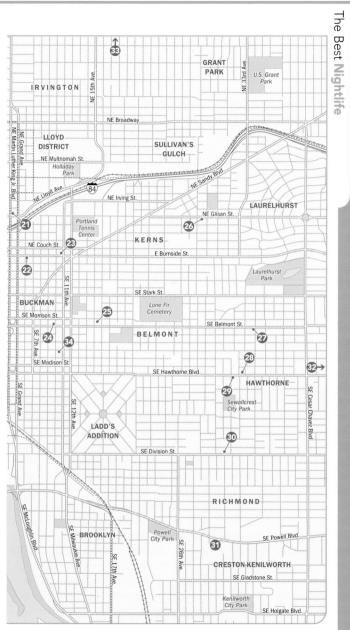

Nightlife Best Bets

Best **View**
★ Departure Lounge, *525 SW Morrison St. (p 115)*; and ★ Portland City Grill, *111 SW 5th Ave. #3000 (p 116)*

Best **Live Jazz**
★★★ Jimmy Mak's, *221 NW 10th Ave. (p 119)*

Best Place **to Catch the Game**
★ Spirit of '77, *500 NE Martin Luther King Jr. Blvd. (p 120)*

Best **Dance Club Experience**
★★ The Escape Nightclub, *333 SW Park Ave. (p 118)*

Best **Sake Selection**
★★ Zilla Sake House, *1806 NE Alberta St. (p 116)*

Best **Martini**
★ Olive or Twist, *925 NW 11th Ave. (p 119)*

Best **Draft Beer Selection**
★★ Bailey's Taproom, *213 SW Broadway (p 115)*

Best **Classy Watering Hole**
★★ The Palm Court, *309 SW Broadway. (p 116)*

Best **for Romantic Snuggling**
★★ Sapphire Hotel, *5008 SE Hawthorne Blvd. (p 116)*

Best **Drag Show**
★★ Darcelle XV Showplace, *208 NW 3rd Ave. (p 118)*

Best **Gaming Experience**
★★ Ground Kontrol Classic Arcade, *511 NW Couch St. (p 119)*

Best **Authentic Old-Portland Brewpub**
★ Tugboat Brewing Company, *711 SW Ankeny St. (p 117)*

Best **Retro Lounge**
★★ Driftwood Room, *729 SW 15th Ave. (p 115)*

Best **Alcohol Alternative**
★ Bula Kava House, *3115 SE Division St. (p 119)*

Retro swank at the Driftwood Room.

Portland Nightlife A to Z

Beer on tap at Bailey's Taproom.

Bars & Lounges

★★ Bailey's Taproom DOWN-TOWN   A great, wide-windowed location downtown and 20 constantly rotating taps (not to mention dozens of bottles) set this place apart from its competitors. *213 SW Broadway (at Ankeny St.).* ☎ *503/295-1004. www.baileystap room.com. MAX: SW 6th & Pine St. Map p 112.*

★ Bazi Bierbrasserie HAW-THORNE   Like Belgian beer? Tripel, Abbey, Delirium Tremens—you name it, this place has it (over 20 on tap at last count), along with Euro-style pub food (Flemish frites!), and sidewalk seating. *1522 SE 32nd Ave. (at Hawthorne Blvd.).* ☎ *503/234-8888. www.bazipdx. com. Bus: 14. Map p 112.*

★ Circa 33 BELMONT   The drinks here focus on the classics—it's named after the year Prohibition was repealed—as well as the cutting edge, with an emphasis on

whiskey. Check out the intimate alleyway seating. *3348 SE Belmont St. (at 34th Ave.).* ☎ *503/477-7682. www.circa33.com. Bus: 15. Map p 112.*

★ Departure Lounge DOWN-TOWN   A little slice of L.A. overlooking downtown, this pop-chic rooftop lounge and Asian-fusion restaurant on top of the Nines hotel has pricey drinks, but the summer views are worth it. *525 SW Morrison St. (at 5th Ave.).* ☎ *503/802-5370. www.departureportland.com. MAX: Pioneer Courthouse/SW 6th Ave. Map p 112.*

★★ Driftwood Room DOWN-TOWN   Preserved from the 1950s, the Hotel DeLuxe's dim little hideaway offers a great happy hour menu and specialty cocktails themed after the Golden Age of Hollywood. Try the violet-hued Elizabeth Taylor. *729 SW 15th Ave. (at Yamhill St.).* ☎ *503/219-2094. MAX: Providence Park. Map p 112.*

The Best Nightlife

★ **Gold Dust Meridian** HAW-THORNE Practically oozing illicit romance, this candlelit place serves scorpion bowls for sharing under a velvet painting of a nude, and boasts the longest happy hour in town (daily 2–8pm). *3267 SE Hawthorne Blvd. (at 32nd Ave.). ☎ 503/239-1143. www.golddustmeridian.com. Bus: 14. Map p 112.*

★★ **The Palm Court** DOWNTOWN Two words sum up the Benson Hotel's grand lobby bar: old school. Stiff bourbon drinks and delish happy hour bites make it a place your grandfather would love, too. Live jazz Tuesday to Saturday evenings. *309 SW Broadway (at Oak St.). ☎ 503/228-2000. Bus: 1, 12, 16, 19, or 94. Map p 112.*

★ **Portland City Grill** DOWNTOWN Arrive early for a window seat to catch the sunset from the 30th floor, and you just might stick around for dinner (steaks and seafood) or some late-evening jazz and flirting. *111 SW 5th Ave. #3000 (at Pine St.). ☎ 503/450-0030. www.portlandcitygrill.com. MAX: SW 5th & Oak St. Map p 112.*

★ **Rontoms** INNER SOUTHEAST Too cool for a sign (look for the helicopter backpack logo), this

mod lounge has a superb back patio with a fire pit and planters, and homemade ice cream on the menu. *600 E Burnside St. (at 6th Ave.). ☎ 503-236-4536. www.rontoms.net. Bus: 12, 19, or 20. Map p 112.*

★★ **Sapphire Hotel** HAWTHORNE No longer the haunt of transient sailors and ladies of the night, this place preserves a maroon, candlelit version of its seamy past, now with food and outstanding cocktails. *5008 SE Hawthorne Blvd. (at 50th Ave.). ☎ 503/232-6333. www.thesapphirehotel.com. Bus: 14. Map p 112.*

★ **Saucebox** DOWNTOWN Nightly DJs transform the bar half of this pan-Asian restaurant into a dark, cacophonous dance club populated by Portland's stylish set. *214 SW Broadway (at Ankeny St.). ☎ 503/241-3393. www.saucebox.com. MAX: SW 6th & Pine St. Map p 112.*

★★ **Zilla Sake House** ALBERTA *Kampai!* This sushi spot stocks dozens of kinds of sake—the largest selection west of the Mississippi, supposedly. They're happy to help you choose the right *junmai ginjo* to go with your dragon roll. *1806*

House Spirits on Distillery Row.

Hopworks serves craft beer in an industrial-chic setting.

NE Alberta St. (at 18th Ave.). ☎ 503/288-8372. www.zillasakehouse.com. Bus: 72. Map p 112.

Breweries & Brewpubs

★ **Cascade Brewing Barrel House** BELMONT Sour beers aged up to a year in wine, port, or whiskey oak barrels are the specialty of this Southeast brewpub—an acquired taste, for sure, but no one does them better. 939 SE Belmont St. (at 10th Ave.). ☎ 503/265-8603. www.cascadebrewingbarrel house.com. Bus: 15. Map p 112.

★★ **Hopworks Urban Brewery** SOUTHEAST Sustainability is a priority here, starting with the organic beers and food, and extending to the recycled materials used in the industrial-ski-lodge setting. Cyclists should steer to their **BikeBar** (3947 N. Williams Ave.; see p 94). 2944 SE Powell Blvd. (at 30th Ave.). ☎ 503/232-4677. www.hop worksbeer.com. Bus: 9. Map p 112.

★ **Lucky Labrador Beer Hall** NORTHWEST Portland's version of a German *bierhaus* occupies a former trucking warehouse complete with a 5-ton crane in the rafters. Dogs and babies are welcome in this casual spot. 1945 NW Quimby St. (at 20th Ave.). ☎ 503/517-4352. www.luckylab.com. Streetcar: NW Northrup & 18th. Bus: 77. Map p 112.

★ **Migration Brewing** NORTH-EAST The ultra-smooth cream ale on the nitro tap is dangerously good at this casual neighborhood brewery, with picnic tables outside and a dartboard inside. 2828 NE Glisan St. (at 29th Ave.). ☎ 503/206-5221. www.migrationbrewing.com. Bus: 17. Map p 112.

★ **Tugboat Brewing Company** DOWNTOWN The oldest microbrewery downtown fits only 50 people and specializes in unfiltered British-style strong ales. Board games and live jazz in the evenings. 711 SW Ankeny St. (at Broadway). ☎ 503/226-2508. MAX: SW 6th & Pine St. Map p 112.

★ **Widmer Brewing** ALBERTA The city's largest craft brewer runs this pub in the semi-industrial zone near the river in North Portland. German food fills the menu, and free brewery tours run on Friday (3pm) and Saturday (11am and 12:30pm). 955 N. Russell St. (at Mississippi Ave.). ☎ 503/281-2437. www.widmerbrothers.com. MAX: Albina/Mississippi. Map p 112.

Cabaret

★★ Darcelle XV Showplace

DOWNTOWN   This campy cross-dressing cabaret has been going since 1967. Get ready for flashy numbers performed by big drag queens, insult comedy, and bachelorette partiers. Shows Wednesday to Saturday. *208 NW 3rd Ave. (at Davis St.).* ☎ *503/222-5338. www.darcellexv.com. Cover $20. Bus: 4, 8, 9, 16, 35, 44, or 77. Map p 112.*

Dance Clubs

★★ The Embers Avenue OLD

TOWN   The old dividing line between gay and straight gets blurred at the Embers Avenue, where everyone comes to dance under flashing lights until the wee hours. *110 NW Broadway.* ☎ *503/222-3082. www.facebook.com/EmbersAvenue. Cover $5–$7 weekends. Bus: 12. Map p 112.*

★★ The Escape Nightclub

DOWNTOWN   Portland's best dance-club experience is an alcohol-free, all-ages, gay-centric extravaganza, open only on Friday and Saturday nights, with floor shows at 2am. The best sound and light system in the city. *333 SW Park Ave. (btw. SW Oak & SW Stark).* ☎ *503/227-0830. Cover $10–$15. Fri, Sat only. Bus: 12. Map p 112.*

★★ Lola's Room DOWNTOWN

This cozy dance spot on the second floor of the historic McMenamin's Crystal Ballroom features DJs and live bands. *1332 W. Burnside.* ☎ *503/225-0047. Cover varies. Bus: 20. Map p 112.*

Gay & Lesbian Bars & Clubs

★ CC Slaughter's OLD TOWN

Popular with a young gay crowd, but definitely hetero-friendly, this nightclub and martini lounge spins different sounds every night of the week. *219 NW Davis St.* ☎ *503/248-9135. www.ccslaughterspdx.com. Bus: 4, 8, 9, 16. Map p 112*

★★ Crush Bar INNER SOUTH-

EAST   Gay-owned and operated, Crush Bar Is a restaurant/bar/events space that welcomes everyone and offers DJs, dancing, and burlesque shows throughout the week. *1400*

Beer!

With more breweries than any other city on Earth and half a dozen annual beer-themed festivals, Portland lays strong claim to being the world's most brew-crazy metropolis. Thank the profusion of local ingredients (especially Willamette Valley hops) and accommodating state laws—but it's mostly due to the sheer enthusiasm and innovation of local brewers, who turn out some of the best lagers, ales, porters, and stouts you'll find anywhere. You could arrange an entire visit just around the city's brewpubs, or take a guided tour of craft breweries aboard the **Brew Bus** ($45, www.brewbus.com) or with **Pubs of Portland** ($30, www.pubsofportlandtours.com). Since it's Portland, you can even group-pedal to local breweries on the **BrewCycle** ($20–$25, www.brewgrouppdx.com) or bring your own brewskies and group-pedal on the Willamette River via the **BrewBarge** ($35, www.brewgrouppdx.com/brewbarge).

The dance floor heats up at Lola's Room.

SE Morrison St. ☎ 503/235-8150. www.crushbar.com. Bus: 12. Map p 112.

★ **Scandals** DOWNTOWN   The only remaining downtown gay bar-restaurant, Scandals has been going strong for over 35 years (10 in this location). It has a DJ booth, pool table, dartboard, and great people-watching. Live local bands and special events on Thursday. *1125 SW Stark St. (at 11th Ave.).* ☎ 503/227-5887. www.scandalspdx. com. Bus: 20. Streetcar: SW 10th and Stark. Map p 112.

Live Jazz & Blues

★★★ **Jimmy Mak's** PEARL Portland's top live jazz club is one of the best in the country, hosting national acts and the outstanding house band led by drummer Mel Brown in an intimate setting. Come for dinner or just the music. *221 NW 10th Ave. (at Everett St.).* ☎ 503/295-6542. www.jimmymaks.com. Cover free to $20. Streetcar: NW 10th & Everett. Map p 112.

Martini Bars

★ **Olive or Twist** NORTHWEST More than just a clever name, this friendly Northwest martini bar serves up classic cocktails, single-malt scotches, and a seemingly endless variety of martinis (try the orange blossom). *925 NW 11th Ave. (at Lovejoy St.).* ☎ 503/546-2900. www.oliveortwistmartinibar.com. Streetcar: NW Lovejoy & 13th. Map p 112.

★ **Vault Martini Bar** PEARL House-made lavender-infused vodka and Marvin Gaye on the stereo are just the tip of the iceberg at this fashionable Pearl watering hole. It's small and can get crowded on weekends with prowling singles. *226 NW 12th Ave. (at Everett St.).* ☎ 503/224-4909. Streetcar: NW 11th & Everett. Map p 112.

Other

★ **Bula Kava House** CLINTON Portland's first kava house serves the mildly narcotic South Pacific beverage in coconut shells. Kava is definitely an acquired taste, but it's quite relaxing (and legal and non-addictive), an alternative social lubricant. *3115 SE Division St. (at 32nd Ave.).* ☎ 503/477-7823. Bus: 4. Map p 112.

★★ **Ground Kontrol Classic Arcade** CHINATOWN   Tired of the same old bar scene? Come

The Best Nightlife

Distillery Row

As if this town needed another alcoholic beverage to excel in, recently 11 microdistilleries have sprung up along "Distillery Row" on SE 7th and 9th avenues, south of Belmont Street. Places like **House Spirits Distillery** (65 SE Washington St, www.housespirits. com, ☎ 503/235-3174), and **New Deal Distillery** (1311 SE 9th Ave., www.newdealdistillery.com, ☎ 503/234-2513) craft small batches of everything from classic gins and brandies to coffee rum and pepper-infused vodka. Most offer tours and tastings. You can take a pedicab tour ($60) or get a $20 "passport" (www.distillery rowtours.com) that covers tasting fees and includes discounts at nearby merchants. More information: www.distilleryrowpdx.com.

here for two floors of classic arcade games and pinball machines, along with a full bar, and DJs in the evenings. *511 NW Couch St. (at 6th Ave.).* ☎ *503/796-9364. www.ground kontrol.com. Free admission. MAX: NW 5th & Couch St. Map p 112.*

Sports Bars
★ **Life of Riley** PEARL   Come cheer the Trail Blazers, Red Sox, or whoever else is playing (well, maybe not the Yankees) at this hard-drinking tavern, a welcome touch of blue collar in the white-collar Pearl. *300 NW 10th Ave. (at Everett St.).* ☎ *503/224-1680. www. lifeofrileytavern.com. Streetcar: NW 10th & Everett. Map p 112.*

★ **Spirit of '77** NORTHEAST Named for the year the Trail Blazers won the championship, this place has high beamed ceilings, a 16-foot-high projection TV, free basketball hoops, and indoor bike parking. *500 NE Martin Luther King Jr. Blvd. (at Lloyd Blvd.).* ☎ *503/232-9977. www. spiritof77bar.com. Bus: 6. Map p 112.*

Wine Bars
★★ **Noble Rot** SOUTHEAST On the third floor of the red

"Rocket" buildings on East Burnside, this wine bar offers wine flights, great views of the city from a glassed-in patio, and dishes using produce from their rooftop garden. *1111 E. Burn-side St. (at 11th Ave.).* ☎ *503/233-1999. www.noblerotpdx.com. Bus: 12, 19, or 20. Map p 112.* ●

Ground Kontrol Classic Arcade.

The Best Arts & Entertainment

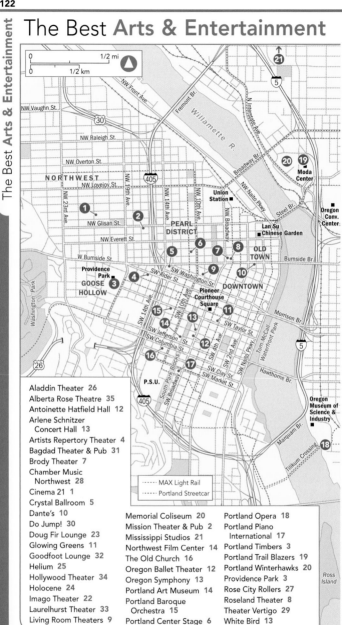

---- MAX Light Rail
---- Portland Streetcar

Previous page: A production of Carmen at the Portland Opera.

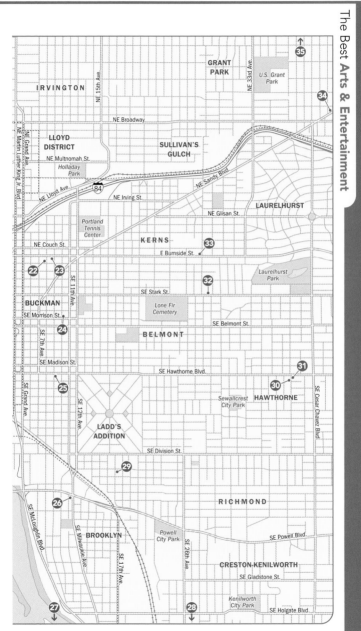

Arts & Entertainment **Best Bets**

Best for a **Beer During a Movie**
★★ Laurelhurst Theater, *2735 E. Burnside St. (p 127)*

Best **Family Entertainment**
★ Do Jump!, *1515 SE 37th Ave. (p 126)*

Best **Popular Music Venue**
★★★ Doug Fir Lounge, *830 E. Burnside St. (p 129)*

Best Place to **Shake Your Booty**
★ Goodfoot Lounge, *2845 SE Stark St. (p 129)*

Best for **Avant-Garde Films**
★★ Northwest Film Center, *1219 SW Park Ave. (p 128)*

Best **Orchestra**
★★★ Oregon Symphony, *1037 SW Broadway (p 125)*

Best for an **Unpredictable Performance**
★ Imago Theater, *17 SE 8th Ave. (p 130)*

Best for a **Belly Laugh**
★★ Helium, *1510 SE 9th Ave. (p 126)*

Best Place to be **Drafted into the Timbers Army**
★ Providence Park, *1844 SW Morrison St. (p 126)*

Best Place for **Glow-in-the-Dark Putting**
★ Glowing Greens, *509 SW Taylor St. (p 128)*

Best **Rough-and-Tumble Entertainment**
★ Rose City Rollers, *7805 SE Oaks Park Way. (p 130)*

Ticket Deals

If you're willing to wait until the day of the show, you can get some good deals on tickets at places like **Portland Center Stage,** which offers any unsold tickets right before curtain time for $20. At the Keller Auditorium, the **Portland Opera** offers unsold tickets to students and active military personnel for $10 and seniors for $20. The **Portland Center for the Performing Arts** has a day-of-show, half-price ticket hotline (☎ 503/432-2960) for performances at the Arlene Schnitzer Concert Hall, Antoinette Hatfield Hall, and Keller Auditorium.

Arts & Entertainment A to Z

Carlos Kalmar conducts the Oregon Symphony.

Classical Music

★★★ Chamber Music Northwest EASTMORELAND
One of the country's oldest chamber music organizations brings a year-round roster of renowned artists to perform at Reed College's Kaul Auditorium and other venues throughout the city. Check website for concert locations. *3203 SE Woodstock Blvd. (and other locations).* ☎ *503/223-3202. www.cmnw.org. Ticket prices vary. Bus: 19. Map p 122.*

★★★ Oregon Symphony
DOWNTOWN Under the baton of music director Carlos Kalmar, the oldest symphony orchestra on the West Coast has become one of the country's top ensembles. Performances are at the Arlene Schnitzer Concert Hall (Sept–May). *1037 SW Broadway (at Main St.).* ☎ *503/228-4294. www.orsymphony.org. Tickets $30–$150. MAX: SW 6th & Madison sts. Bus: 8, 9, 10, 14, 17, or 66. Map p 122.*

★★★ Portland Baroque Orchestra
DOWNTOWN Under the inspired leadership of Monica Huggett, this ensemble performs baroque and classical music composed before 1840, often on original instruments, at the First Baptist Church (on Sundays at Reed College's Kaul Auditorium). *909 SW 11th Ave. (at Taylor St.).* ☎ *503/222-6000. www.pbo.org. Tickets $25–$54. Streetcar: SW 11th & Taylor. Map p 122.*

★★★ Portland Piano International
DOWNTOWN The world's leading pianists and up-and-coming stars of the keyboard perform solo recitals in Lincoln Hall at Portland State University. *Lincoln Hall (PSU), 1620 SW Park (at Market).* ☎ *503/228-1388. www.portlandpiano.org. Tickets $25–$100. Streetcar: SW Park & Market. Map p 122.*

Comedy Clubs

★ Brody Theater
CHINATOWN Swing by for a stand-up or improv

show or an avant-garde theater production; come back later and take a class. *16 NW Broadway (at Burnside).* ☎ *503/224-2227. www. brodytheater.com. Tickets $8–$12. MAX: SW 6th & Pine St. Bus: 1, 12, 19, 20, 54, or 56. Map p 122.*

★★ **Helium** INNER SOUTHEAST Local and national stand-up acts appear at this slick comedy club. *1510 SE 9th Ave. (at Hawthorne Blvd.).* ☎ *888/643-8669. www.helium comedy.com. Tickets $5–$35, 2-item minimum. Bus: 10 or 14. Map p 122.*

Concert & Event Venues

★ **Alberta Rose Theatre** ALBERTA Catch some live music, an independent film, or a taping of the *Live Wire!* radio show at this 300-seat restored 1927 movie house. *3000 NE Alberta St. (at 30th Ave.).* ☎ *503/719-6055. www. albertarosetheatre.com. Tickets $15– $28. Bus: 72. Map p 122.*

★★ **Antoinette Hatfield Hall** DOWNTOWN This striking building encloses the classic Newmark and high-tech Dolores Winningstad theaters, hosting plays, dance, music, films, and more. *1111 SW Broadway (at 11th Ave.).* ☎ *503/248-4335. www.pcpa.com. Ticket prices vary. MAX: SW 6th & Madison St. Bus: 8, 9, 10, 14, 17, or 66. Map p 122.*

★★★ **Arlene Schnitzer Concert Hall** DOWNTOWN The crown jewel of the Portland Center for the Performing Arts, the "Schnitz" is the city's most lavish performance space, home to the Oregon Symphony and a year-round roster of top performers and performances. *1037 SW Broadway (at Main St.).* ☎ *503/248-4335. www.pcpa.com. Ticket prices vary. MAX: SW 6th & Madison St. Bus: 8, 9, 10, 14, 17, or 66. Map p 122.*

★ **Memorial Coliseum** LLOYD DISTRICT The former home of the Trail Blazers now hosts the Portland Winterhawks (see p 130), big-ticket shows (despite horrendous acoustics), and the kickoff of the Rose Festival Grand Floral Parade. *300 N. Winning Way.* ☎ *503/797-9619. www.rosequarter.com. Ticket prices vary. MAX: Interstate/Rose Quarter. Bus: 35. Map p 122.*

★★ **The Old Church** DOWN-TOWN Every Wednesday at noon, this 1883 Carpenter Gothic landmark hosts free "sack lunch" concerts of classical music by local artists. Other concerts and events through the year. Also see p 45 *1422 SW 11th Ave.* ☎ *503/222-2031. www.oldchurch.org. Free admission. Streetcar: SW 11th & Clay. Map p 122.*

★ **Providence Park** DOWN-TOWN This historic open-air stadium hosted Elvis and 14,000 screaming fans in 1957; now it's home base for the Portland State University Vikings football team and the Portland Timbers MLS team (see p 129). *1844 SW Morrison St. (at 18th Ave.).* ☎ *503/553-5400. www. providenceparkpdx.com. Ticket prices vary. MAX: Providence Park. Bus: 15, 18, 20, 51, or 63. Map p 122.*

Dance

★ **kids Do Jump!** HAWTHORNE With energetic performances that are as much aerial acrobatics as dance, this inventive local company always puts on a good show. *1515 SE 37th Ave. (at Hawthorne Blvd.).* ☎ *503/231-1232. www.dojump.org. Ticket prices vary. Bus: 14. Map p 122.*

★ **Oregon Ballet Theater** DOWNTOWN This company, founded in 1989, performs both classical (including a yearly *Nutcracker*) and modern ballet at the Newmark Theatre in Antoinette Hatfield Hall (above) and the Keller

White Bird hosts international dance companies such as Momix.

Auditorium (222 SW Clay St.) *1111 SW Broadway (at 11th Ave).* ☎ *503/222-5538. www.obt.org. Tickets $15–$140. MAX: SW 6th & Madison St. Bus: 8, 9, 10, 14, 17, or 66. Map p 122.*

★★ **White Bird** DOWNTOWN Fans of international modern dance should check out what's being produced by White Bird. Venues change but the main performance site is Arlene Schnitzer Concert Hall. *1037 SW Broadway.* ☎ *503/245-1600. www.whitebird.org. Ticket prices vary. Bus: 8, 9, 10, 14, 17, or 66. Map p 122.*

Film

★★ kids **Bagdad Theater & Pub** HAWTHORNE This 1927 theater with a pub and two bars shows second-run movies for cheap, along with offbeat performances. *3702 SE Hawthorne Blvd.* ☎ *503/467-7521. www.mcmenamins.com. Ticket prices vary. Bus: 14. Map p 122.*

★ **Cinema 21** NORTHWEST One of Portland's most beloved movie theaters shows shorts, documentaries, and critically acclaimed features that won't make it to the multiplex. *616 NW 21st Ave. (at Irving St.).* ☎ *503/223-4515. www.cinema21.com. Tickets $8–$10. Bus: 17. Map p 122.*

★ **Hollywood Theater** HOLLYWOOD The city's most ornate classic theater retains its 1926 Byzantine rococo facade and shows independent and foreign films. *4122 NE Sandy Blvd. (at 41st Ave).* ☎ *503/281-4215. www.hollywoodtheatre.org. Tickets $5–$7. Bus: 12. Map p 122.*

★★ **Laurelhurst Theater** LAURELHURST Pizza, salads, microbrews, and second-run flicks fill the bill at this restored 1923 theater with an awesome neon sign. *2735 E. Burnside St. (at 28th Ave).* ☎ *503/232-5511. www.laurelhursttheater.com. Tickets $5–$8. Bus: 20. Map p 122.*

★★ **Living Room Theaters** DOWNTOWN Combine a European lounge and cafe with an independent theater and you get the chicest eat-in-your-seat movie house in town. *341 SW 10th Ave. (at Stark St.).* ☎ *971/222-2010. http://pdx.livingroomtheaters.com. Tickets $8–$10. Bus: 20. Streetcar: SW 10th & Stark. Map p 122.*

★ **Mission Theater & Pub** NORTHWEST This former church and longshoreman's union hall hosts first-run films, live music, talks, and sporting events. Snag a balcony seat. *1624 NW Glisan St. (at*

The Portland Opera performs at Keller Auditorium.

17th Ave.). ☎ 503/223-4527. www. mcmenamins.com. Tickets $3–$6. Bus: 20. Map p 122.

★★ Northwest Film Center

DOWNTOWN The Portland Art Museum's Whitsell Auditorium hosts classic, experimental, animated, foreign, and indie films, plus film festivals and work by local filmmakers. *1219 SW Park Ave. (at Madison St.).* ☎ *503/221-1156, ext. 10. www.nwfilm.org. Tickets $8–$10. Streetcar: Art Museum. Map p 122.*

Minigolf

★ Glowing Greens DOWN-

TOWN And now for something completely different: pirate-themed, glow-in-the-dark miniature golf, in the basement of the downtown Hilton. *509 SW Taylor St. (at 5th Ave.).* ☎ *503/222-5554. www.glowing greens.com. Tickets $5–$11. MAX: Pioneer Courthouse Sq. Map p 122.*

Opera

★★ Portland Opera INNER

EASTSIDE The Rose City's opera company puts on five productions (Sept–Mar) at Hampton Opera Center and at Keller Auditorium (222 SW Clay St.), including works by Puccini, Mozart, Verdi, Wagner, Strauss, Leonard Bernstein, and Philip Glass. *211 SE Caruthers St.* ☎ *503/241-1407. www.portland opera.org. Tickets $45–$150. Streetcar: SE Water/OMSI. Map p 122.*

Popular Music

★★ Aladdin Theater SOUTH-

EAST This 1920s vaudeville house is now a stellar mid-size performance hall for live music from Emmylou Harris to Maceo Parker and Ryan Adams. *3017 SE Milwaukie Ave.* ☎ *503/233-1994. www.aladdin-theater.com. Tickets $10–$45. Bus: 9, 17, 19, 66, or 70. Map p 122.*

★ Crystal Ballroom DOWN-

TOWN When's the last time you rocked out to Modest Mouse on the floating-on-ball-bearings dance floor of a 1914 ballroom? Jimi Hendrix, James Brown, and the Grateful Dead all played at this local institution; Rudolf Valentino did the tango here in the 1920s. *1332 W. Burnside St. (at 14th Ave.).* ☎ *503/225-0047. www.danceonair.com. Ticket prices vary. Bus: 20. Map p 122.*

★ Dante's OLD TOWN The Sin-

ferno Cabaret, Karaoke From Hell, live bands, and DJs make this club a tempting destination for a night of dancing and debauchery. *350 W. Burnside St. (at 5th Ave.).* ☎ *503/226-6630. www.danteslive.com. Cover* free to $20. Bus: 12, 19, or 20. Map p 122.

★★★ **Doug Fir Lounge** INNER SOUTHEAST   Attached to the Jupiter Hotel, the Doug Fir features alt-rock and great acoustics. *830 E. Burnside St. (at 9th Ave.).* ☎ *503/ 231-9663. www.dougfirlounge.com. Cover $8–$25. Bus: 12, 19, or 20. Map p 122.*

★ **Goodfoot Lounge** LAUREL-HURST   Get up offa that thing and shake it to jazz, funk, soul, Afrobeat, and everything in between. *2845 SE Stark St. (at 29th Ave.).* ☎ *503/239-9292. www.thegoodfoot.com. Cover free to $10. Bus: 15. Map p 122.*

★ **Holocene** SOUTHEAST   Booty Basement and Snap '90s Night are just two of the regular events at this nightclub, featuring DJs and live music on two stages, with a dance floor and cheap covers. *1001 SE Morrison St. (at 10th Ave.).* ☎ *503/ 239-7639. www.holocene.org. Cover $5–$10. Bus: 15. Map p 122.*

★★ **Mississippi Studios** MISSIS-SIPPI   This venue in the heart of the historic Mississippi District caters to people who actually want to *listen* to live music in an intimate setting. Good acoustics, and free

shows once a month. *3939 N. Mississippi Ave. (at Shaver St.).* ☎ *503/ 288-3895. www.mississippistudios. com. Cover free to $18. Bus: 4. Map p 122.*

★ **Roseland Theater** CHINA-TOWN   Not the most pleasant live-music venue, but one of the few non-stadium places to see major rock acts. *8 NW 6th Ave. (at Burnside St.).* ☎ *503/224-8499. www.roseland pdx.com. Ticket prices vary. Bus: 9, 17, 20, 54, or 56. Map p 122.*

Sports

★★★ **Portland Timbers** DOWNTOWN   The Major League Soccer team fills Providence Park stadium with the howls of the "Timbers Army" (Mar–Oct). *1844 SW Morrison St. (at 18th Ave.).* ☎ *503/ 53-5400. www.portlandtimbers.com. Tickets $18–$35. MAX: Providence Park. Map p 122.*

★ **Portland Trail Blazers** ROSE QUARTER   The Northwest's only NBA team last won the championship in 1977, but they still sell out the 20,000-seat Moda Center arena (Nov–Apr). *1 Center Court.* ☎ *503/ 234-9291. www.nba.com/blazers. Tickets average $60. MAX: Moda Center. Map p 122.*

Rocking out at the Doug Fir Lounge.

The Portland Timbers play at Providence Park.

★ **Portland Winterhawks** ROSE QUARTER   This junior hockey team, part of the Western Hockey League, counts Hall of Famers Cam Neely and Mark Messier among its NHL alumni (Memorial Coliseum, Sept–Mar). *300 N. Winning Way.* ☎ *503/238-6366. www.winterhawks. com. Tickets $14–$51. MAX: Moda Center. Map p 122.*

★ **Rose City Rollers** SELLWOOD The Breakneck Betties and the Axles of Annihilation are two of the six teams that make up this all-female amateur roller derby league. At Oaks Park in Sellwood (Jan–June). *7805 SE Oaks Park Way.* ☎ *503/784-1444. www.rosecityrollers.com. Tickets $16–$22. Bus: 70. Map p 122.*

Theater

★ **Artists Repertory Theater** DOWNTOWN   More challenging contemporary productions, along with works by established playwrights like Harold Pinter and David Mamet, come courtesy of this first-rate company. *1516 SW Alder St. (at 16th Ave.).* ☎ *503/241-1278. www. artistsrep.org. Tickets $25–$50. MAX: Providence Park. Bus: 15, 20. Map p 122.*

★ kids **Imago Theater** INNER SOUTHEAST   You never know what a night with Imago holds— physical comedy, animal costumes, mime, dance, acrobatics, music— but it definitely will be interesting. Productions like Frogz, ZooZoo, and Splat are as entertaining to kids as they are to their parents. *17 SE 8th Ave. (at Burnside St.).* ☎ *503/231-9581. www.imagotheatre.com. Ticket prices vary. Bus: 12, 19, or 20. Map p 122.*

★★ **Portland Center Stage** PEARL   The Gerding Theater at the Armory is home of the city's largest professional theater company, performing classic and contemporary works and musicals (Sept–June). *128 NW 11th Ave. (at Davis St.).* ☎ *503/445-3700. www. pcs.org. Tickets $20–$65. Bus: 12, 19, or 20. Map p 122.*

★ **Theatre Vertigo** BELMONT Performing at the Shoebox Theater, this small but talented company puts on three intriguing ensemble performances every season; Thursday you pay what you will. *2110 SE 10th Ave.* ☎ *503/306-0870. www. theatrevertigo.org. Tickets $15. Bus: 15. Map p 122.* ●

Downtown & Northwest Hotels

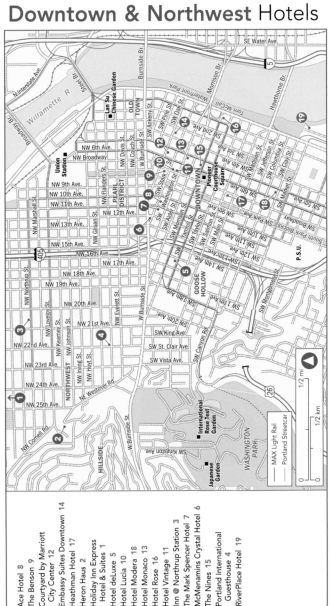

Previous page: The Benson Hotel.

East Side Hotels

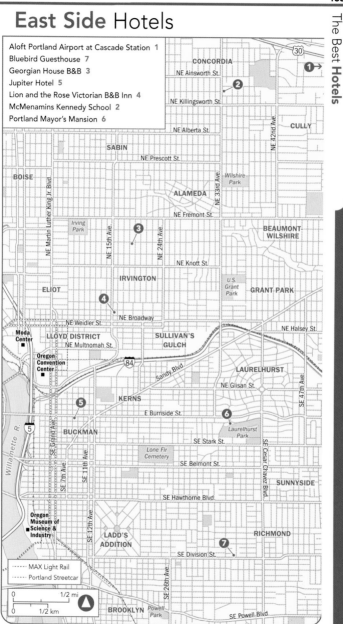

Hotel Best Bets

Best for **Families**
★ Embassy Suites Downtown $$$ *319 SW Pine St. (p 135)*

Best **Value**
★ Portland International Guesthouse $ *2185 NW Flanders St. (p 138)*

Best **Historic B & B**
★★★ Portland Mayor's Mansion $$ *3360 SE Ankeny St. (p 138)*

Best **Splurge**
★★★ The Nines $$$ *525 SW Morrison St. (p 138)*

Best for **Romance**
★ Lion and the Rose Victorian B&B Inn $$ *1810 NE 15th Ave. (p 137)*

Best **Service**
★★ Heathman Hotel $$$ *1001 SW Broadway (p 135)*

Best **Unusual Vibe**
★★★ McMenamins Kennedy School $$ *5736 NE 33rd Ave. (p 138)*

Best **Hotel Restaurant**
★★★ Hotel Modera $$ *515 SW Clay St. (p 136)*

Best **Hip Vibe**
★★ Ace Hotel $$ *1022 SW Stark St. (p 135)*

Best for **Convenience to the Airport**
★ Aloft Portland Airport at Cascade Station $$ *9920 NE Cascades Pkwy. (p 135)*

Best for **Willamette River Views**
★★ RiverPlace Hotel $$$ *1510 SW Harbor Way (p 138)*

Best for **Traditional Elegance**
★★★ The Benson $ *309 SW Broadway (p 135)*

Best for **Live Music**
★ Jupiter Hotel $ *800 E. Burnside (p 137)*

The lobby of the Ace Hotel.

Hotels A to Z

★★ Ace Hotel DOWNTOWN
Stylish from the photo booth in the lobby to the turntables in the rooms, the Ace is a short walk from Powell's City of Books and is surprisingly affordable, befitting a hip young clientele (and their pets). *1022 SW Stark St. 503/228-2277. www.acehotel.com/portland. 79 units. Doubles $145–$250. AE, MC, V. Streetcar: SW 10th & Stark. Map p 132.*

★ Aloft Portland Airport at Cascade Station AIRPORT Way more chic than your average airport hotel, Aloft boasts large, loft-inspired rooms, free parking, and an overall mod design aesthetic. *9920 NE Cascades Pkwy. 503/200-5678. www.aloftportlandairport.com. 136 units. Doubles $99–$239. AE, MC, V. MAX: Cascades Station. Map p 133.*

★★★ The Benson DOWNTOWN Since 1912, the Benson has topped Portland's old-world-charm category, now updated with Tempur-Pedic mattresses. Put it this way: Obama stayed here. *309 SW Broadway. 888/523-6766 or 503/228-2000. www.bensonhotel.com. 287 units. Doubles $159–$359. AE, MC, V. MAX: SW 5th & Oak. Map p 132.*

★ kids Bluebird Guesthouse SOUTHEAST Rooms named after famous writers (and Elliott Smith) fill a cozy 1910 Arts and Crafts house within walking distance of the Clinton and Division street action. *3517 SE Division St. 866/717-4333 or 503/238-4333. www.bluebirdguesthouse.com. 7 units. Doubles $70–$135 w/ breakfast. AE, MC, V. Bus: 4. Map p 133.*

★ Courtyard by Marriott City Center DOWNTOWN A solid midrange option in the heart of the city, this Courtyard was freshly created from a former office building and has a friendly, contemporary feel. *550 SW Oak St. 800/606-3717 or 503/505-5000. www.myfavoritecourtyard.com. 256 units. Doubles $109–$315. AE, MC, V. MAX: SW 5th & Oak. Map p 132.*

★ kids Embassy Suites Downtown DOWNTOWN Mostly two-room suites, perfect for families, fill this historic property. Enjoy a good free breakfast and walk to everything in downtown. *319 SW Pine St. 800/EMBASSY [362-2779] or 503/279-9000. www.embassyportland.com. 276 units. Doubles $149–$289 w/breakfast. AE, MC, V. MAX: SW 5th & Oak. Map p 132.*

★ Georgian House Bed & Breakfast IRVINGTON This B&B occupies a historic home befitting its tree-lined neighborhood; owner Willie is a gracious host who whips up a filling breakfast. *1828 NE Siskiyou St. 503/281-2250. www.thegeorgianhouse.com. 4 units. Doubles $113–$165 w/breakfast. AE, MC, V. Bus: 8. Map p 133.*

★★ Heathman Hotel DOWNTOWN Adjacent to "the Schnitz" concert hall, you'll find a first-rate place with classic service and modern amenities, from in-room French press coffeemakers to a library full of signed first editions. *1001 SW Broadway. 800/551-0011 or 503/241-4100. http://portland.heathmanhotel.com. 150 units. Doubles $219–$450. AE, MC, V. Bus: 15 or 31. Map p 132.*

★ Heron Haus NORTHWEST Stay in a historic English Tudor mansion within walking distance of Forest Park and Northwest 21st and

A suite at Hotel Lucia.

23rd avenues. *2545 NW Westover Rd.* ☎ *503/274-1846. www.heron haus.com. 6 units. Doubles $135–$195 w/breakfast. AE, MC, V. Bus: 18. Map p 132.*

★ **Holiday Inn Express Hotel & Suites** NORTHWEST Nothing fancy, just a good value at the north end of 23rd Avenue, near where the shopping district veers west on NW Thurman Street. *2333 NW Vaughn St.* ☎ *503/484-1100. www.holiday innexpress.com. 90 units. Doubles $129–$250 w/breakfast. AE, MC, V. Bus: 15, 17, or 77. Map p 132.*

★★ **Hotel deLuxe** DOWNTOWN Step into the Golden Age of Hollywood at this reinvented historic downtown hotel decorated with black-and-white photos of classic stars. Rooms can be snug, but they have a breezy LA aesthetic. The cozy Driftwood Room has been a Portland cocktail staple since the 1950s. *729 SW 15th Ave.* ☎ *866/986-8085 or 503/219-2094. www.hoteldeluxeportland.com. 103 units. Doubles $159–$299. AE, MC, V. MAX: Providence Park. Map p 132.*

★★★ **Hotel Lucía** DOWNTOWN Paintings by Northwest artists and photos by former White House photog David Hume Kennerly set an artsy, contemporary tone and draw a younger professional crowd (and their pets) to this centrally located downtown hotel. *400 SW Broadway.* ☎ *866/986-8086 or 503/225-1717. www.hotellucia.com. 128 units. Doubles $149–$309. AE, MC, V. MAX: Oak/SW 1st. Map p 132.*

★★★ **Hotel Modera** DOWNTOWN Outstanding eatery Nel Centro with its outdoor firepits and vertical wall garden are just one facet of this stylish luxury boutique hotel fashioned from a 1950s motor lodge. *515 SW Clay St.* ☎ *503/484-1084. www.hotelmodera.com. 174 units. Doubles $159–$259. AE, MC, V. MAX: Mall/SW 5th. Map p 132.*

★ **Hotel Monaco** DOWNTOWN Pet-friendly, centrally located, over-the-top room decor—the Monaco, part of the Kimpton chain, is all this, plus it offers free evening wine tastings. *506 SW Washington St.* ☎ *888/207-2201 or 503/222-0001. www.monaco-portland.com. 221 units. Doubles $159–$359. AE, MC, V. MAX: Mall/SW 5th. Map p 132.*

★ **Hotel Rose** DOWNTOWN A great value for a downtown riverside hotel, this newly revamped motor lodge has small rooms with extra-comfy beds and unbeatable access to Waterfront Park. *50 SW Morrison St.* ☎ *8866/866-7977 or 503/221-0711. www.hotelrose portland.com. 140 units. Doubles $179–$359. AE, MC, V. MAX: SW Yamhill. Map p 132.*

★★ Hotel Vintage DOWNTOWN
Another Kimpton offering, the historic and freshly refurbished Hotel Vintage (built in 1894) boasts garden spa suites, stylish decor, a free evening wine tasting, and Pazzo Italian restaurant. *422 SW Broadway.* ☎ *800/263-2305 or 503/228-1212. www.hotelvintage-portland.com. 117 units. Doubles $159–$379. AE, MC, V. MAX: Pioneer Square. Map p 132.*

★ Inn @ Northrup Station
NORTHWEST A colorful retro retreat right on the streetcar line, this all-suite boutique hotel has lots of rooms with balconies and make-your-own waffles for breakfast. *2025 NW Northrup St.* ☎ *800/224-1180 or 503/224-0543. www.northrup station.com. 70 units. Doubles $139–$239 w/breakfast. AE, MC, V. Streetcar: NW Northrup & 22nd. Map p 132.*

★ Jupiter Hotel SOUTHEAST
You'll feel like an indie rock star at this eco-friendly, youth-centric boutique motel with its chalkboard doors and illuminated wall panels—and you can catch a real rock star at the attached Doug Fir Lounge. *800 E. Burnside St.* ☎ *877/800-0004 or 503/230-9200. www.jupiterhotel.com.*

80 units. Doubles $139–$189. AE, MC, V. Bus: 12, 19, or 20. Map p 133.*

★ Lion and the Rose Victorian B&B Inn IRVINGTON This 1905 Queen Anne building is stocked with antiques and claw-foot tubs, but the best part may be what's outside: a beautiful rose garden and the eminently walkable Irvington neighborhood. *1810 NE 15th Ave.* ☎ *800/955-1647 or 503/287-9245. www.lionrose.com. 8 units. Doubles $135–$215 w/breakfast. AE, MC, V. Bus: 8. Map p 133.*

★ kids The Mark Spencer Hotel
DOWNTOWN This favorite downtown budget choice for extended stays features clean, comfortable rooms with kitchenettes. *409 SW 11th Ave.* ☎ *800/548-3934 or 503/224-3293. www.markspencer.com. 102 units. Doubles $159–$279. AE, MC, V. MAX: Galleria/SW 10th. Map p 132.*

★ McMenamins Crystal Hotel
DOWNTOWN A true rock-'n'-roll hotel across the street from the century-old Crystal Ballroom, this recently refashioned building has an underground soaking pool, live music at the cellar bar, and tickets to ballroom shows. *303 SW 12th*

The McMenamin's Mini-Empire

Local brothers Mike and Brian McMenamin opened **Produce Row Café** (see p 107) in 1974. Since then, they've expanded to almost 60 historic hotels, brewpubs, movie theaters, and music venues across Oregon and Washington. Each of the properties bears the distinctive McMenamin's stamp: lovingly restored historic buildings decorated with whimsical art and paintings. Their many pubs are fully stocked with their own line of microbrews—they're one of the Northwest's largest craft distillers. In Portland they run numerous theater-pubs such as the **Mission** (p 127) and the **Bagdad** (p 127), along with the **Kennedy School Hotel** (below), the **Crystal Hotel** (above), and the historic **Crystal Ballroom** (p 128). For more info, see **www.mcmenamins.com**.

Ave. ☎ 503/972-2670. www.
mcmenamins.com/crystalhotel. 51
units. Doubles $115–$195. AE, MC,
V. Bus: 20. Map p 132.

★★★ kids **McMenamins Kennedy School** ALBERTA Sleep in
a former schoolroom, complete
with blackboard, or just roam the
art-paneled halls of this former elementary school. Restaurant, movie
theater, and soaking pool on site.
5736 NE 33rd Ave. ☎ 888/249-3983
or 503/249-3983. www.mcmenamins.
com/427-kennedy-school-home. 35
units. Doubles $135–$185. AE, MC,
V. Bus: 73. Map p 133.

★★★ **The Nines** DOWNTOWN
From its eighth-floor atrium lobby
to its rooftop Departure Lounge,
the Nines is fun, fashionable, and
full-service; rooms have a turquoise-
and-white color scheme and great
downtown city views. Urban Farmer
is the best hotel restaurant in town.
525 SW Morrison St. ☎ 877/229-
9995 or 503/715-1738. www.thenines.
com. 331 units. Doubles $259–$559.
AE, MC, V. MAX: Pioneer Courthouse. Map p 132.

★ **Portland International
Guesthouse** NORTHWEST

Six spotless rooms share three
full bathrooms at this friendly
guesthouse in a quiet residential
neighborhood; best budget accommodation in Portland. 2185 NW
Flanders St. ☎ 877/228-0500 or
503/224-0500. www.pdxguesthouse.
com. 6 units. Doubles $70–$80. AE,
MC, V. Bus: 15. Streetcar: NW 21st &
Lovejoy. Map p 132.

★★★ **Portland Mayor's Mansion** LAURELHURST Built in 1912
for a former mayor of Portland, this
imposing Colonial Revival is a feast
of period detail located right on
historic Laurelhurst Park. 3360 SE
Ankeny St. ☎ 503/232-3588. www.
pdxmayorsmansion.com. 4 units.
Doubles $175–$280. MC, V. Bus: 75.
Map p 133.

★★ **RiverPlace Hotel** DOWNTOWN The only truly riverside
hotel downtown, this upscale, pet-
friendly Kimpton property abuts
Waterfront Park. 1510 SW Harbor
Way. ☎ 800/227-1333 or 503/228-
3233. www.riverplacehotel.com. 84
units. Doubles $189–$459. AE, MC,
V. Streetcar: SW 1st & Harrison. Map
p 132. ●

The former Portland Mayor's Mansion is now a chic B&B.

Mount Hood

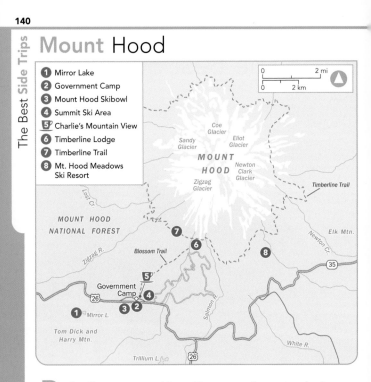

1. Mirror Lake
2. Government Camp
3. Mount Hood Skibowl
4. Summit Ski Area
5. Charlie's Mountain View
6. Timberline Lodge
7. Timberline Trail
8. Mt. Hood Meadows Ski Resort

Portland's snow-capped icon shimmers on the eastern horizon whenever the skies are clear. At 11,240 feet, the stratovolcano Mount Hood is Oregon's highest point, with year-round skiing on the Palmer Glacier—one of twelve glaciers on Mount Hood—above the classic Timberline Lodge. The road there, U.S. 26, is a National Scenic Byway that generally traces the historic Barlow Road, the final stretch of the Oregon Trail. START: **Troutdale, I-84 exit 18, 17 miles east of Portland.**

❶ ★ **kids** **Mirror Lake.** A trailhead on Hwy. 26 between mileposts 51 and 52 accesses an easy 1.6-mile trail to a picture-perfect lake with spectacular views of Mt. Hood. A Northwest Forest Pass ($5/day per car) is required to park at the trailhead.

❷ ★ **Government Camp.** First settled in 1900, this tiny mountain resort community sits at the foot of Mt. Hood amid fir and cedar forests. It has a handful of restaurants, hotels, and rental condos, making it a good base in summer or winter.

❸ ★ **kids** **Mount Hood Skibowl.** The closest ski resort to Portland is also the country's largest night ski area, with 600 acres lit up after dark. The Cascade Express lift

Previous page: Vista House at Crown Point, overlooking the Columbia River Gorge.

accesses popular cruising terrain and panoramic views from 7,300 feet. It's as much a summer destination as a winter one, with an adventure park and mountain-bike rentals. *87000 E. Hwy. 26, Government Camp.* ☎ *503/272-3206. www.skibowl.com. Lift tickets $53 adults, $49 children 6–12 & seniors 59 and over.*

④ ★ kids Summit Ski Area.

Also near Government Camp, the Northwest's first ski resort—opened in 1927—has a single lift and two downhill runs. It also offers snow tubing and 10 miles of cross-country ski trails. *90255 E. Government Camp Loop, Government Camp.* ☎ *503/272-0256. www.summitski area.com. Lift tickets $30 adults, $20 children 6–12, seniors over 70 & kids 5 & under free.*

What ⑤ **Charlie's Mountain View** lacks in ambience it makes up for in good food, such as the Mountain Cheese Burger with waffle fries, and the wide-window view of Mt. Hood. *88462 E. Government Camp Loop, Government Camp.* ☎ *503/272-3333. www.charlies mountainview.com. $.*

⑥ ★★★ Timberline Lodge.

Built as a WPA project in the 1930s, this mountain lodge is full of classic Cascadian character, from its huge stone fireplace and glass tile mosaics to the extensive carved woodwork. You might recognize it from the film *The Shining,* where it stood in for the snowy exterior of the fictional Overlook Hotel. The attached ski area, with 41 trails and nine lifts, is the only one in the country with year-round skiing. *Timberline Hwy., Mt. Hood.* ☎ *800/547-1406 or 503/272-3410. www.timberlinelodge.com. Rooms $145–$375. Lift tickets $66 adults, $27 kids 6–12 & adults over 59, $5 kids under 6.*

⑦ ★ Timberline Trail. You can

take it 40.7 miles all the way around the mountain or just do part on a day hike, but either way this is one of Oregon's most scenic hiking trails. *Access from Timberline Lodge or Mount Hood Meadows. Snow-free mid-July through early Oct.*

⑧ ★★★ kids Mt. Hood Meadows Ski Resort. The biggest

resort on the mountain is also one of the best in the Northwest for serious skiers, with 2,150 acres of wildly varied terrain, nine freestyle parks, and a full ski school. Locals know to head to Heather Canyon and Elk and Yoda Bowls on powder days. *14040 Hwy 35.* ☎ *503/659-1256. www.skihood.com. Lift tickets $79 adults, $39 juniors 7–14 & seniors 64 and over, $9 kids 7 and under.*

Snowcapped Mount Hood.

Columbia River Gorge

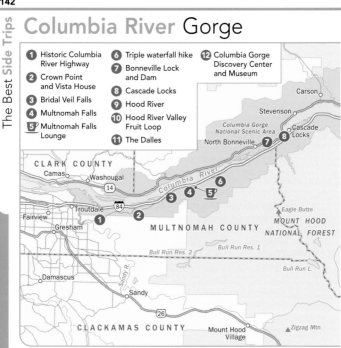

1. Historic Columbia River Highway
2. Crown Point and Vista House
3. Bridal Veil Falls
4. Multnomah Falls
5. Multnomah Falls Lounge
6. Triple waterfall hike
7. Bonneville Lock and Dam
8. Cascade Locks
9. Hood River
10. Hood River Valley Fruit Loop
11. The Dalles
12. Columbia Gorge Discovery Center and Museum

The Northwest's version of the Grand Canyon is 85 miles of basalt cliffs, lofty waterfalls, lush forests, and, oh yes, the fourth-largest river in the U.S. Much of this National Scenic Area is still as wild as it was when Lewis and Clark paddled through. The Oregon side of the Gorge is a must-do day trip—or longer—from Portland. Combine it with Mt. Hood (p 140) for an even more impressive excursion. START: **Troutdale, OR, 17 miles east of Portland.**

① ★★★ Historic Columbia River Highway. The best (although not the fastest) way to experience the grandeur of the Columbia River Gorge is the way they did it in the days of Model Ts. Built between 1916 to 1926, the country's first scenic highway was designed as a way for car travelers to enjoy the magnificent scenery, and it was considered one of the great engineering feats of its time. The narrow road winds for 70 miles along the southern side of the gorge, with dramatic climbs and descents and S-curves, past one amazing viewpoint, roaring waterfall, and 2,000-foot cliff to the next. Many of the original Florentine viaducts crafted by Italian stonecutters are still in place. Leave at least a few hours—better yet a whole day—from Troutdale to reach the Dalles (see p 147), or just Hood River (see p 145). If you're in a hurry, I-84 also runs along the river. ☎ 541/308-1700. www.fs.usda.gov/crgnsa.

SKAMANIA
COUNTY

WASHINGTON

White
Salmon

KLICKITAT
COUNTY

Hood River **9**

84

Mosier 30

Lyle

14

Columbia Gorge
National Scenic Area

Odell

12

35

Hood
River

10

The Dalles **11**

HOOD
RIVER
COUNTY

OREGON

Mill Cr.

Fivemile Cr.

WASCO COUNTY

Eightmile Cr.

Dufur

MOUNT
HOOD

Fifteenmile Cr.

197

Elk Mtn.   Lookout Mtn.

0   10 mi

0   10 km

② ★★★ **Crown Point and
Vista House.** If the Columbia
Gorge had a headquarters, it would
be at Crown Point, with its 30-mile
views from atop a sheer 733-foot
cliff. Here you'll find the unmistakable octagonal Vista House, built in
1918 as an observatory and rest

stop. Since then its resume has
expanded to include a museum
and gift shop, and it recently
enjoyed a $3.2-million restoration. *3
miles east of Corbett on Historic
Columbia River Hwy., I-84 exit 22.*
☎ *503/695-2240. www.vistahouse.
com. Vista House open 9am–6pm*

Vista House offers panoramic views of the Columbia River Gorge.

daily Apr–Oct; 10am–4pm Fri–Sun Nov–Mar, weather permitting. Free admission.

3 ★ kids **Bridal Veil Falls.** Five miles east of Crown Point, Bridal Veil Creek tumbles down Larch Mountain and plunges into space, falling in two gauzy plumes for a total of 120 feet. Two trails leave from the picnic tables and restrooms at the parking lot. The short and easy lower trail heads down to the base, while a longer interpretive trail winds up to the lip of the falls, with log fences for the clumsy and agoraphobic. Both trails are under 1 mile round-trip. *Milepost 28 on Historic Columbia River Scenic Highway, I-84 exit 28. Open daily dawn–dusk. Free admission.* ☎ *800/551-6949.*

4 ★★ kids **Multnomah Falls.** Oregon's highest cascade, and the second-highest year-round waterfall in the country, plummets a total of 620 feet in two tiers at the bottom of Larch Mountain. It's a majestic sight, even though its tourist must-see status can bring big crowds on weekends. The scene is enhanced, or at least not marred, by the graceful curve of the Benson Footbridge, built in 1914 about 100 feet over the lower falls. It's part of a 1.2-mile trail that climbs 600 feet to the top of the upper falls, where an expansive panorama and the much smaller "Little Multnomah" waterfall await. Direct any questions to the information center inside the Multnomah Falls Lodge (below). *I-84 exit 31.* ☎ *503/ 695-2372. Open daily dawn–dusk; information center daily 9am–5pm. Free admission.*

Recharge with a bite at the historic **5** **Multnomah Falls Lodge** at the base of the falls, built in 1925. Look for an outdoor table in the summer, but don't bother asking

Multnomah Falls.

about overnight accommodations; there aren't any. *All meals daily.* ☎ *503/695-2376. www.multnomah fallslodge.com. $$.*

6 ★★ kids **Triple waterfall hike.** With 77 cascades on the Oregon side of the Gorge (in case you were wondering, that's Washington on the other side), picking which ones to visit can be tough. A relatively easy 4-mile loop trail hits no fewer than three, including an optional fourth, all without climbing over 800 feet. Start at the Horsetail Falls Trailhead on the Columbia River Highway. After ogling 176-foot **Horsetail Falls,** take Trail #400 up a mossy slope to reach 80-foot **Ponytail Falls,** which have undercut the hillside so much that the trail leads behind them. From here you'll climb a bit farther to cross a bridge over the upper end of narrow Oneonta Gorge, before reaching a side trail (#438) that climbs almost a mile to **Triple Falls,** spilling over 100 feet into a large pool. Come back down to Trail #400 and take a left to descend to the Oneonta Gorge Trailhead. From here you can walk east along the highway half a mile back to your car—or else, if you're properly outfitted with waterproof waders, and limber enough to climb over slippery fallen logs, take the stairs down into cool, deep Oneonta Gorge and wade upstream 1,000 feet to **Oneonta Falls.** *Horsetail Falls Trailhead on the Columbia River Highway, 1½ miles east of I-84 exit 35.*

7 ★ kids **Bonneville Lock and Dam.** Completed in 1936 for hydropower and river navigation, this massive dam stretches 3,460 feet across the Columbia. Four sections connect both banks and three islands, one of which holds the **Bradford Island Visitors Center,** where you can watch through underwater windows as native salmon migrate upstream from October through December. (Fish ladders were added later.) The California sea lions that congregate at the base of the dam gobble so many fish that wildlife officials sometimes have to relocate them. Next to the dam, the **Bonneville Fish Hatchery** (☎ 541/374-8393) raises Chinook, Coho, and steelhead salmon and has display ponds where you can feed rainbow trout and white sturgeon. (Don't miss 10-foot-long Herman the Sturgeon, who's over 60 years old.) *I-84 exit 40.* ☎ *541/374-8820. www.nwp. usace.army.mil/locations. Visitor center open daily 9am–5pm; fish hatchery daily 7:30am–dusk. Free admission.*

8 ★ **Cascade Locks.** A series of rapids kept steamboats from ascending the Columbia past this point until a series of locks were blasted from solid stone in 1896. Forty-two years later, most of them have disappeared beneath the rising waters of Lake Bonneville, behind Bonneville Dam. The upper locks are still above water, though, and are part of **Cascade Locks Marine Park,** with a visitor center, a small museum on river history, and

the Oregon Pony, the first steam engine in the West. It's the home base of the **Columbia Gorge Sternwheeler** (☎ 503/224-3900 or 800/224-3901; www.sternwheeler. com), a three-deck paddle-wheeler that gives tours of the gorge. You can cross to Washington on the **Bridge of the Gods** ($1 toll) named after a natural bridge that once stood here according to Native American legend. It's open to cars and foot traffic, including hikers on the Pacific Crest Trail. *I-84 exit 44.* ☎ *541/374-8619. www.cascade locks.net. Visitor center open May–Sept, hours vary; museum open Mon–Fri noon–5pm, Sat & Sun 10am–5pm May–Sept. Free admission.*

9 ★★ **Hood River.** The "Aspen of windsurfing" owes its worldwide reputation to the regular winds that rush down the gorge, sometimes topping 30mph in the summer. In fact, Hood River is an all-around adventure-sports hotspot, with kayaking, mountain biking, and hiking galore in the gorge and the nearby slopes of Mt. Hood. At night and on the rare calm day, there are plenty of shops and eateries to explore.

Fish ladder at Bonneville Dam.

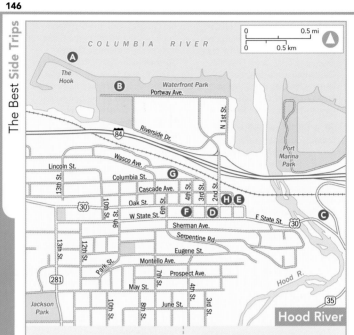

Hood River

You can watch windsurfers and kiteboarders leap whitecaps from **The Hook,** a short protected harbor, and the adjacent **B Water-front Park,** both on the opposite (river) side of I-84 from town. If you're inspired to give either a try, stop by **C Windance Sailboards** (108 Hwy. 35 at Hwy. 30; ☎ 541/386-2131; www.windance.com) for rentals and lessons. (Keep in mind that learning here is like learning to drive in Manhattan: difficult, but then you're ready for anything.) To take on one of the many mountain-bike trails on the flanks of Mt. Hood to the south, head to **D Discover Bicycles** (210 State St.; ☎ 541/386-4820; www.discoverbicycles.com)

for tips and the largest rental selection in the Northwest. The bulk of the town's restaurants are on or near Oak Street (U.S. 30), including **E Celilo Restaurant and Bar** (16 Oak St.; ☎ 541/386-5710; www.celilorestaurant.com) and **F Kaze Sushi** (212 4th St.; ☎ 541/387-0434). One notable exception is the **G Full Sail Tasting Room & Pub** (506 Columbia St.; ☎ 541/386-2247; www.fullsailbrewing.com), one of Oregon's first and most famous craft breweries. If all this makes you want to spend the night, the 100-year-old **H Hood River Hotel** (102 Oak St.; ☎ 800/386-1859; www.hoodriverhotel.com) is the city's oldest and one of its best.

❿ ★★ kids Hood River Valley Fruit Loop. The river valley between the Columbia and Mt. Hood packs a lot into a small and

scenic area: wineries, beehives, lavender farms, and 2.4 million fruit trees, almost a quarter of Oregon's total. (It's the country's top

Mount Hood Railroad

Experience a bit of time travel aboard a 1906-era railroad through the Hood River Valley. Started as a freight line, it still pulls the occasional freight car but is mostly used for scenic tours to Odell (2 hr. round-trip) and Parkdale (4 hr. round-trip). It's worth it to splurge for the upper dome car, and pack a lunch for the short stopovers. Along the way you'll get views of Mt. Hood and the gorge, and experience one of the few switchback tracks still in use in the U.S. Special tours throughout the year range from brunch and Murder Mystery dinner trains to Western Robbery rides and a holiday Polar Express. ☎ 800/872-4661. www.mthoodrr.com. Trains run year-round Tues–Sun, schedule varies, regular excursions $30–$55 adults, $25–$35 children, meal trains and special excursions $30–$82 per person.

pear-growing district.) A 35-mile loop drive along Hwy. 281 and Hwy. 35, through the burgs of Dee, Odell, Oak Grove, Pine Grove, and Mount Hood, is a wonderful way to spend a day meandering from one farm, roadside produce stand, and alpaca ranch to another. (An organized driving route counts 36 stops.) Many farms let you pick your own fruit, and festivals from spring through fall celebrate what's in season, from cherries in July to pumpkins in November. *Maps and information at Hood River visitor center, I-84 exit 64.* ☎ *541/386-2000 or 800/366-3530. www.hoodriverfruit loop.com. Fruit tree blossoms peak in Apr, fall foliage in Oct.*

⓫ ★ **The Dalles.** The eastern end of the Columbia River Highway is a historic city at one of the few spots along the river where early traders could load boats and Oregon Trail pioneers could raft their way to Oregon City, the end of the trail. It's full of 19th-century buildings and more recent murals. The **Fort Dalles Museum** (500 W. 15th St.; ☎ 541/296-4547; www.fort dallesmuseum.org), Oregon's

oldest, occupies the surgeon's quarters of an 1856 fort. In the mid-1800s, Methodist missionaries preached to Native Americans from **Pulpit Rock,** still standing at 12th and Court streets.

⓬ ★★ **Columbia Gorge Discovery Center and Museum.** Everything you ever wanted to know about the gorge, from the Ice Age and Lewis and Clark through the finer points of how to windsurf, comes together in this exceptional museum. The wide-windowed building itself is a wonder, and its collection spans geology, natural history, and 12,000 years of human habitation, with films, photos, and artifacts. Living history exhibits and a live raptor program round out the experience. Outside, a paved trail connects wetlands, a pond, and viewpoints of the gorge, and continues 4.5 miles to the Dalles. *5000 Discovery Dr.* ☎ *541/296-8600. www.gorgediscovery.org. Open daily 9am–5pm. Admission $9 adults, $7 seniors, $5 children 6–16, free for 6 and under.*

Willamette Valley Wine Tour

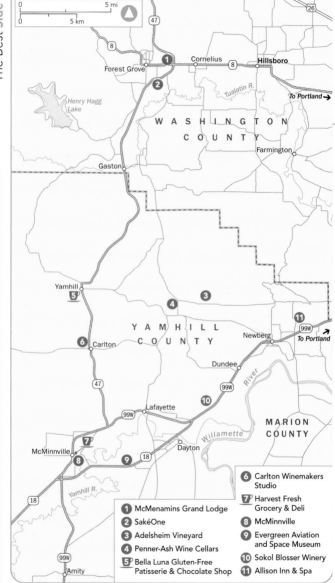

0   5 mi
0   5 km

Cornelius   **Hillsboro**

Forest Grove

Tualatin R.

To Portland →

Henry Hagg Lake

W A S H I N G T O N
C O U N T Y

Farmington

Gaston

Yamhill

Y A M H I L L
C O U N T Y

Carlton

Newberg   *To Portland →*

Dundee

Lafayette

M A R I O N
C O U N T Y

Willamette River

McMinnville

Dayton

Yamhill R.

Amity

1 McMenamins Grand Lodge
2 SakéOne
3 Adelsheim Vineyard
4 Penner-Ash Wine Cellars
5 Bella Luna Gluten-Free Patisserie & Chocolate Shop
6 Carlton Winemakers Studio
7 Harvest Fresh Grocery & Deli
8 McMinnville
9 Evergreen Aviation and Space Museum
10 Sokol Blosser Winery
11 Allison Inn & Spa

The fertile, sheltered valley of the Willamette ("wih-LAM-it") River, the "promised land" for so many settlers on the Oregon Trail, is now one of the country's top winegrowing regions. It's a kind of anti-Napa, with little of the pretentiousness or crowds, although summer weekends can get very busy. Pinot noir is gospel here, but you'll find other cool-weather vintages as well, including pinot gris, Rieslings, Gewürztraminers, and ever-improving chardonnays. You'll also find roadside produce stands and farms growing everything from tulips to hazelnuts. (*Be warned:* Hwy. 99W can get choked with traffic on weekends, so consider an alternate route.) START: **U.S. 26 west to OR 47, about 27 miles from Portland to Forest Grove.**

Wine tasting at Adelsheim Vineyard.

➊ ★ McMenamins Grand Lodge. One of the, well, grandest properties in the McMenamins portfolio, this 1922 retirement home is full of all the kaleidoscopic artwork, comfy lounges, and craft beer you'd expect, along with a wine bar, spa, movie theater, soaking pool, and four on-site choices for food and libations. There's even a disc golf course on the expansive lawns that surround the property. The less expensive guestrooms have shared bathrooms. *3505 Pacific Ave., Forest Grove. ☎ 877/ 922-9533 or 503/992-9533. www. mcmenamins.com/GrandLodge. Rooms $65–$175 double. AE, MC, V.*

➋ ★ SakéOne. Leave it to Oregon to have the only American-owned craft sake brewery in the world. After a tour of the facilities, head to the tasting room to sample their popular blue-bottled Momokawa line, as well as the fruit-infused Moonstone and undiluted "G" brands. *820 Elm St. off OR 47, Forest Grove. ☎ 800/550-SAKE (7253) or 503/357-7056. www.sake one.com. Tasting room open daily 11am–5pm; tasting flights $5–$15 per person.*

➌ ★ Adelsheim Vineyard. One of Oregon's most popular pinot noir producers, Adelsheim has a big tasting room and a patio overlooking the vineyard. Tastings aren't cheap, but you can sample vintages that aren't on the market—including some outstanding single-vineyard wines—and the fee goes toward purchases. *16800 NE Calkins Lane, Newberg. ☎ 503/538-3652. www.adelsheim.com. Tasting room open daily 11am–4pm. Fee $15. Tour by appointment only.*

4 ★★ **Penner-Ash Wine Cellars.** It's a bit tricky to find, but winemaker Lynn Penner-Ash's winery offers outstanding vintages and wonderful views from a hilltop between Yamhill and Newberg. The pinot noirs and Syrahs are deservedly famous, but they also make viogniers, rubeos, Rieslings, and rosés. *15771 NE Ribbon Ridge Rd., Newberg. ☎ 503/554-5545. www.pennerash.com. Tasting room open Wed–Sun 11am–5pm. Fees $15. Tour by appointment only.*

Anyone who's on a gluten-free diet will be happy to stop in at **5** **Bella Luna Gluten-Free Patisserie & Chocolate Shop** for a gluten-free sweet. *185 S. Maple St., Yamhill, OR. ☎ 503/662-0098. www.bellaluna patisserie.com. $.*

6 ★★ **Carlton Winemakers Studio.** Eleven vintners banded together here under one roof offer tastings of up to 40 different wines. If you're pressed for time or just like to sample a wide range, it's a good choice to visit. The modern building was the first in the country to be certified by the U.S. Green Building Council. *801 N. Scott St., Carlton. ☎ 503/852-6100. www.winemakersstudio.com. Tasting room open daily 11am–5pm. Fee $5–$20.*

Stock up for your winery picnic lunch at **7** **Harvest Fresh Grocery & Deli,** a natural food store offering local produce, sandwiches, salads, and fresh-squeezed juices and smoothies. *251 NE 3rd St., McMinnville. ☎ 503/472-5740. www.harvestfresh.com. $.*

8 ★ **McMinnville.** Amble down 3rd Street, "Oregon's Favorite Main Street," to find local shops, boutiques, wine-tasting rooms, and top-notch restaurants. *Bon Appétit* magazine dubbed McMinnville one of the country's best small towns for food lovers, and you can see why at places like **Thistle** (228 NE Evans St.; ☎ 503/472-9623; www.thistle restaurant.com) and **Bistro Maison**

A spa treatment at the luxe Allison Inn.

(729 NE 3rd St.; ☎ 503/474-1888; www.bistromaison.com). Even the breakfast spots are four-star: Try the pork meatloaf at the **Crescent Café** (526 NE 3rd St.; ☎ 503/435-2655; www.crescentcafeonthird.com). The rooftop bar and deck at the **McMenamins Hotel Oregon** (310 NE Evans St.; ☎ 888/472-8427 or 503/472-8427; www.mcmenamins.com/HotelOregon) is a perfect stop at the end of a wine tour day. (The tater tots are a guilty pleasure.)

⑨ ★★★ kids Evergreen Aviation and Space Museum. In between bites of brie and sips of Syrah, how about a side trip to see the largest plane ever built? Howard Hughes's "Spruce Goose," a wooden flying boat with a 320-foot wingspan, flew exactly once, for 1 minute, before ending up at this hangarlike museum alongside fighter jets, stunt planes, a Mercury space capsule, and much more. There's also an IMAX theater and a waterpark with a wave pool and ten waterslides—including four that start from inside a real 747 plopped on the roof. *500 NE Capt. Michael King Smith Way, McMinnville.* ☎ *503/434-4185. www.evergreenmuseum.org. Museum admission $25 adults, $24 seniors over 63, $23 children 5–16, free for children under 5.*

Waterpark admission $32, or $27 if under 42 inches tall. Museum open daily 9am–5pm; waterpark daily 10am–8pm.

⑩ ★★ Sokol Blosser Winery. Whites are the favorites at this popular Dundee winery, the first in the country to receive LEED certification for sustainable practices. Tour the vineyards in a custom biodiesel ATV to see organic farming techniques and a 24kW solar array in action. *5000 Sokol Blosser Lane, Dundee.* ☎ *800/582-6668 or 503/864-2282. www.sokolblosser.com. Tasting room open daily 10am–4pm. Fee $15. Tours by appointment only.*

⑪ ★★ Allison Inn & Spa. The only high-end getaway in Wine Country makes an excellent base for wine touring. Rooms are huge, with HDTVs and (in some) hot tubs, and the lush grounds are perfect for strolling and sipping your latest purchase. Relax in the spa and enjoy topnotch wine-country cuisine at the Jory restaurant. What really earns raves, though, is the attentive but unobtrusive service. *2525 Allison Lane, Newberg.* ☎ *503/554-2525. www.theallison.com. Rooms $375–$405.*

Oregon Coast

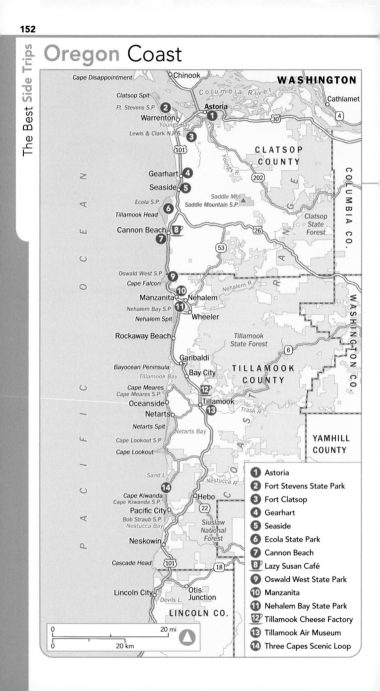

1 Astoria
2 Fort Stevens State Park
3 Fort Clatsop
4 Gearhart
5 Seaside
6 Ecola State Park
7 Cannon Beach
8 Lazy Susan Café
9 Oswald West State Park
10 Manzanita
11 Nehalem Bay State Park
12 Tillamook Cheese Factory
13 Tillamook Air Museum
14 Three Capes Scenic Loop

The northern part of Oregon's coastline gets the most visitors, and it's easy to see why: The thickly forested Coast Range mountains meet the crashing waves of the Pacific in towering headlands and wide, flat beaches punctuated by towering, off-shore rock monoliths. Yes, it's too cold to swim without a wet suit; but summers are uncrowded by California or East Coast standards, and winter brings its own stormy beauty—plus migrating gray whales. And thanks to a forward-thinking 1967 law, all of Oregon's breathtaking coastline is forever public. START: **U.S. 30 West from Portland, 100 miles.**

Astoria Column tops Coxcomb Hill.

❶ ★★ **Astoria.** The oldest American settlement west of the

Mississippi was founded as Fort Astoria in 1811 by fur trappers working for John Jacob Astor, America's first multimillionaire. Today, restored Victorian homes pepper the hillsides, and restaurants, art galleries, and shops are revitalizing the dilapidated downtown. Spend an afternoon strolling the riverwalk, watching cruise ships and barges pass and sea lions lounge on piers. While you're there, grab a vegetarian crepe or a plate of local seafood at the charming **Columbian Café** (1114 Marine Dr.; ☎ 503/325-2233; www.columbian voodoo.com). For more of a workout, climb the staircase inside the 125-foot-high **Astoria Column** atop Coxcomb Hill for a panoramic view. Don't miss the outstanding **Columbia River Maritime Museum** (1792

The wreck of the Peter Iredale, in Fort Stevens State Park.

Marine Dr.; ☎ 503/325-2323; www. crmm.org), with exhibits on the history of the country's second-largest river and the wreck-strewn "Graveyard of the Pacific" at its mouth. If you're inspired to stay, the **Cannery Pier Hotel** (10 Basin St.; ☎ 888/ 325-4996 or 503/325-4996; www. cannerypierhotel.com) is a modern luxury hotel built on an old cannery pier stretching 600 feet out in the river. *www.astoriaoregon.com.*

❷ ★ **Fort Stevens State Park.** This 4,200-acre park in Oregon's far northwestern corner is guarded by a fort built during the Civil War to protect the mouth of the Columbia River. It was the only military installation in the continental U.S. to be fired on by the Japanese during World War II—17 shells in June 1942, to be exact. Now it consists of a military museum surrounded by huge concrete bunkers and paths for hiking and bicycling. There's also a lake for swimming and a large campground with yurts and cabins. Head to the park's Pacific beach to find the rusted wreck of the *Peter Iredale,* a four-masted steel sailboat that ran ashore on October 25, 1906. Living history events happen from April to September, including a Civil War reenactment over Labor Day weekend. *8 miles from Astoria via U.S. 101 & Ridge Rd.* ☎ *503/861-1671 or 800/551-6949. www.oregonstate parks.org/park_179.php. Museum open 10am–6pm summer and fall; 10am–4pm winter and spring. Admission $5 per car. Campsites $21; yurts $55; cabins $89–$99.*

❸ ★★★ **kids** **Fort Clatsop— Lewis and Clark National Historic Park.** After slogging across half of North America, Lewis and Clark spent the cold, rainy winter of 1805–06 holed up in a log stockade they built near present-day Astoria. Named after the friendly local

Clatsop Indians, the reconstructed fort is part of the Lewis and Clark National and State Historical Parks group. The primitive buildings give an accurate and atmospheric picture of the conditions at the fort over 200 years ago. In the summer, costumed interpreters demonstrate frontier-era skills such as making candles and shooting a flintlock rifle. From here the 6.5-mile **Fort to Sea Trail** leads through forest, dunes, and fields to **Sunset Beach State Recreation Area.** *Off U.S. 101, 5 miles southwest of Astoria.* ☎ *503/861-2471. www.nps.gov/ lewi. Admission $5 adults, free for ages 16 and under. Mid-June to Labor Day daily 9am–6pm; Labor Day to mid-June daily 9am–5pm.*

❹ ★ **Gearhart.** If your goal is to get away from it all, even by Oregon Coast standards, then this tiny beach town is for you. Beyond a scant handful of tourist-oriented businesses, Gearhart is just private homes—expensive ones—and a nearly deserted 4-mile stretch of beach. At the **Gearhart Ocean Inn** (67 N. Cottage Ave.; ☎ 503/738-7373; www.gearhartoceaninn.com), you can steam your own clams in the kitchenette or walk across the street to the cozy **Pacific Way Bakery & Café** (601 Pacific Way; ☎ 503/738-0245) for a croissant or French dip sandwich. Next door is **Pop's Sweet Shop** (567 Pacific Way; ☎ 503/738-8484), serving dozens of flavors of Tillamook ice cream. Head to the end of Wellington Street at the south end of town to find a short, unmarked trail to the **Necanicum River estuary,** often packed with shore birds stalking the mudflats for dinner. From here, the Pacific dunes are just a short walk west.

❺ ★ **kids** **Seaside.** Oregon's version of the Jersey Shore brings a little tacky fun to the otherwise staid

Coastline views in Ecola State Park.

beach towns around here. The town itself is full of historic cottages dating to the turn of the 20th century, but what draws most visitors is the wide white-sand beach and the 2-mile beachfront promenade, lined with souvenir shops, video arcades, minigolf courses, and amusement-park rides. Lifeguards are on duty throughout the summer, making this a popular beach with families. There are plenty of places to buy kites or rent three- and four-wheeled beach cycles. At the **Seaside Aquarium** (200 N. Promenade; ☎ 503/738-6211; www.seasideaquarium.com), one of the oldest on the West Coast, you can touch a sea anemone or feed a seal. *80 miles from Portland via U.S. 26. www.seasideor.com.*

⑥ ★★★ Ecola State Park. Lewis and Clark arrived here in 1806—the farthest south they ventured on the Oregon coast—to buy whale blubber and see a whale washed up on the beach. Their 16-year-old Indian guide, Sacagawea, was in the scouting party. You can trace part of their route on a 2.5-mile loop trail through steep forests of Sitka spruce, or take a slightly longer trail 600 feet up to the top of Tillamook Head, which Clark called "the steepest worst & highest mountain I ever ascended." (It's not that bad, and the views of the coastline are more than worth it.) More hiking trails lead to the beach, a primitive hike-in campsite, and picnic areas on high bluffs, perfect for spotting whales in the winter and spring— and surfers year-round. *Just north of Cannon Beach on U.S. 101. ☎ 800/ 551-6949 or 503/436-2844. www. oregonstateparks.org/park_188.php. Fee $5 per vehicle.*

⑦ ★★★ Cannon Beach. Named for a cannon that washed ashore from a shipwreck in 1846, Cannon Beach may be the prototypical Oregon coast town, full of homes covered in weathered cedar shingles, plus art galleries, shops, and good restaurants and hotels. Visitors pack the place in the summer, but it hasn't turned into a northwest Carmel-by-the-Sea quite yet. Iconic **Haystack Rock** is a 235-foot-high sea stack (formed by wave erosion) just off the beach, home to sea birds like tufted puffins. It's surrounded by tide pools full of life—just don't get stranded by the rising tide. Follow up an intimate seafood dinner at **Newmans at 988** (988 S. Hemlock St.; ☎ 503/436-1151; www.newmansat 988.com) with a night at the **Stephanie Inn** (2740 S. Pacific St.; ☎ 800/633-3466 or 503/436-2221; www.stephanie-inn.com), regularly listed among the most romantic in Oregon. The **Inn at Cannon Beach** (3215 S. Hemlock St.; ☎ 800/321-6304; www.atcannonbeach.com) is off the main drag but near the beach, with oceanfront balcony rooms overlooking Haystack Rock. *80 miles from Portland via U.S. 26.* www.cannonbeach.org.

Enjoy a marionberry scone at 🟨 **8** **Lazy Susan Café.** This two-story Cannon Beach cottage is one of the best breakfast spots in town. They're also open for lunch and dinner, with salads, sandwiches, and seafood stews. *126 N. Hemlock St.* ☎ *503/436-2816. $. No credit cards.*

🟨 **9** ★★ **Oswald West State Park.** Mountains meet the sea in a show-stopping way at this coastal park. A 15-minute hike to the secluded, crescent-shaped beach keeps out most of the crowds, except for surfers, who love the constant waves. More trails lead to viewpoints from the headlands on either side, and the Oregon Coast Trail goes up and over 1,600-foot **Neahkahnie Mountain.** Translated as "place of the supreme deity" in the native Tillamook language, the mountain is reputed to hide a lost Spanish fortune that has cost more than one treasure-hunter's life. One trailhead is just south of the park boundary on U.S. 101. From there, it's 2 steep miles through dense forest to the summit. *10 miles south of Cannon Beach.* ☎ *800/551-6949.* www.oregonstateparks.org/park_ 195.php. *Fee $5 per vehicle.*

Cannon Beach's iconic Haystack Rock.

Strolling on the beach at Manzanita.

⑩ ★★★ Manzanita. A favorite getaway on the northern Coast, this 600-person village has one main street and not much to do besides eat, sleep, and go to the beach. It's close enough to Cannon Beach and numerous state parks to enjoy those by day, but all you can hear at night are the waves. The **Ocean Inn at Manzanita** (32 Laneda Ave.; ☎ 866/368-7701 or 503/368-7701; www.oceaninnatmanzanita.com) has 10 condo and kitchenette units right on the sand, and the **Coast Cabins** (635 Laneda Ave.; ☎ 800/435-1269 or 503/368-7113; www.coastcabins.com) are five cedar cottages with a Japan-meets-Scandinavia aesthetic. The **Bread and Ocean Bakery** (154 Laneda Ave.; ☎ 503/368-5823; www.breadand ocean.com) is one of the better lunch and dinner places in town, with great cinnamon rolls and sandwiches. *14½ miles south of Cannon Beach on U.S. 101. www.explore manzanita.com.*

⑪ ★ Nehalem Bay State Park. This park covers most of the sandy spit separating Nehalem Bay and the mouth of the Nehalem River from the ocean. You'll find a campground, rental yurts, and paths for horses, bikes, and joggers. In summer, guided horseback rides are available for anywhere from 1 hour to all day. Or go crabbing, fishing, or sailing around the calm waters of the bay, paddle a sea kayak upriver, or head offshore for surfing or windsurfing. Some parts of the beach may be closed to protect nesting seabirds. ☎ 503/368-5154 or 800/551-6949. www.oregonstate parks.org/park_201.php. Fee $5 per car; yurts $44–$54; horseback rides $70–$150 per person for 1–2 hours, full day $400.

After a tour of **⑫ Tillamook Cheese Factory,** which produces 167,000 pounds of cheese every day, you can sample the goods at the attached store, including cheese curds (aka "squeaky cheese"), ice cream, and fudge. *4175 Hwy. 101 N. ☎ 800/542-7290 or 503/815-1300. www.tillamook. com/cheese-factory. $.*

⑬ ★ kids Tillamook Air Museum. More than 30 restored vintage planes and helicopters have found a home in the world's largest free-standing wooden building, a former World War II Navy blimp hangar that stands over 15 stories high. The collection includes

The Cape Meares Lighthouse.

a P-38 Lightning, a P51-Mustang, and a Bf-109 Messerschmitt. *6030 Hangar Rd.* ☎ *503/842-1130. www. tillamookair.com. Admission $9 adults, $8 seniors over 63, $5 youth 5–17, free for 5 and under. Open daily 9am–5pm.*

⓮ ★★★ **Three Capes Scenic Loop.** Perhaps the prettiest drive on this part of the coast, this 30-mile route takes you from Tillamook to Pacific City, past view after view of the rugged coast. Take 3rd Street out of Tillamook toward the ocean and turn right on Bayocean Road to reach **Cape Meares State Scenic Viewpoint,** home to Oregon's largest Sitka spruce and the **Cape Meares Lighthouse** (☎ 503/842-2244; www.capemeareslighthouse.org). The 200-foot-high headland is the only place in the U.S. where you can see three

National Wildlife Refuges at once: Cape Mears, Oregon Islands, and Three Arch Rocks. Look for peregrine falcons and gray whales in the winter. Keep going to **Cape Lookout State Park** (☎ 503/842-4981 or 800/551-6949; www.oregonstateparks.org/park_186.php), where a 2.5-mile trail winds through dense old-growth rainforest to the tip of the peninsula, a great place to spot gray whales. There's also a campground (sites $21) with yurts ($44–$54), cabins ($98) and a $5 entry fee per car. Past Oceanside and Netarts Bay, **Cape Kiwanda State Natural Area** (☎ 800/551-6949; www.oregonstateparks.org/park_180.php) consists of sea cliffs, a beach, and a giant sand dune popular with hang gliders. Another giant sea stack looms offshore. ●

The Savvy Traveler

Before You Go

Tourist Offices

The **Travel Portland Visitor Information Center** in Pioneer Courthouse Square downtown (701 SW 6th Ave.; ☎ 503/275-8355 or 877/678-5263; www.travelportland.com) is open Monday through Friday 8:30am to 5:30pm, Saturday 10am to 4pm, and Sunday 10am to 2pm from May through October. For destinations outside the city, contact the **Oregon Tourism Commission,** 670 Hawthorne St. SE, Suite 240, Salem, OR 97301 (☎ 800/547-7842; www.traveloregon.com).

The Best Times to Go

The start of summer—defined locally as July 5, when the clouds finally retreat—is gorgeous in Portland and all of Oregon, for that matter. Sunshine replaces drizzle, lawns go from deep green to dry brown, and temperatures are warm, but usually not uncomfortably so. From June through September, it's highly advisable to book hotel and car reservations ahead of time—as far ahead as possible for weekends, holidays, and events like the Rose Festival. Spring and fall are more of a crapshoot, weather-wise, but you might hit a week or even two of sunshine, and gardens in Portland are at their lushest. Prices fall and reservations open up in these seasons, and even more so in the winter, except for the holidays.

Festivals & Special Events

SPRING   April brings the **Spring Beer & Wine Fest** (www.springbeerfest.com), filling the Convention Center with craft microbrews, regional wines, spirits, food, crafts, and music. This is also the month to catch the **Tulip Festival** at Wooden Shoe Tulip Farm in Woodburn (☎ 503/634-2243 or 800/711-2006; www.woodenshoe.com), whose fields of vibrant blooms will make you feel as if you're in Holland, not 35 miles south of Portland.

May starts with the **Cinco de Mayo Fiesta** (www.cincodemayo.org), supposedly the country's largest, which celebrates Portland's sister-city status with Guadalajara, Mexico. Food, entertainment, and music are all on the bill in Governor Tom McCall Waterfront Park. At the end of the month, the **Mother's Day Rhododendron Show** at Crystal Springs Rhododendron Garden, SE 28th Avenue and Woodstock Boulevard (☎ 503/771-8386), is a riot of blossoming rhododendrons and azaleas.

SUMMER   June is the month of extended events, led by the **Portland Rose Festival** (☎ 503/227-2681; www.rosefestival.org), the city's oldest (started in 1888) and biggest. Three weeks of events include the **Rose Festival Grand Floral Parade,** a starlight parade, the election of the Rose Queen, a waterfront carnival, and dragon boat races on the river. Some of the events are even free.

The middle of the month also sees the 3-week **Pedalpalooza** (www.shift2bikes.org/pedalpalooza), an only-in-Portland festival of all things bike-related. Hundreds of events are held, most of them free, including the immense **World Naked Bike Ride**—we're talking thousands of bicyclists in the buff. The **Portland Pride Festival and Parade** (www.pridenw.org) happens over a weekend in mid-June, with a Pride Parade on Sunday, live

Previous page: Mirror Lake near Mt. Hood.

entertainment, a drag race (heels, not wheels), and pet parade.

Over the extended Fourth of July weekend, the **Waterfront Blues Festival** (☎ 503/282-0555; www.waterfrontbluesfest.com) fills Governor Tom McCall Waterfront Park with 4 days of national head-liners. Sponsored by Safeway and benefitting the Oregon Food Bank, it's the largest blues festival west of the Mississippi.

The last full weekend in July brings more beer, this time in the form of the 4-day **Oregon Brewers Festival** (☎ 503/778-5917; www.oregonbrewfest.com), one of the largest and oldest craft-beer festi-vals in the U.S. Waterfront Park is the setting for close to 100 craft brewers from home and abroad, with demonstrations, exhibits, food, and live music.

In late July, indie music fans flock to **PDX Pop Now!** (www.pdxpopnow.com), a free, all-ages festi-val of local music featuring upwards of 50 artists selected by public vote. When the 3-day event is over, you can take home a two-CD compilation.

Mid-August's **The Bite of Oregon** (www.biteoforegon.com), a fundraiser for Special Olympics Oregon, features food and wine samples from local chefs and regional wineries, along with live music, cooking demos, and other entertainment. Mid-August is also time for another distinctively local happening: the **Providence Bridge Pedal** (☎ 503/281-9198; http://blog.bridgepedal.com), in which 10 of the city's bridges are partly closed to make room for cyclists. Choose from routes ranging from 13 to 36 miles (or a 5-mile walk) and enjoy amazing views that zip by through a car window the other 364 days of the year.

Summer also brings many local street fairs on the east side of the city, mostly 1-day affairs with food and drink vendors, music, crafts, and the occasional bouncy castle. The list includes the **Mississippi Street Fair** in early July (www.mississippiave.com); the **Division and Clinton Street Fair** in late July (www.divisionclinton.com); the **Alberta Street Fair** in mid-August (www.albertamainst.org/street-fair); the **Hawthorne Street Fair** in late August (www.thinkhawthorne.com/happenings); and the **Belmont Street Fair** in mid-September (www.belmontdistrict.org/street-fair).

FALL   In early September, **Musicfest NW** (www.musicfestnw.com) fills Waterfront Park and the clubs of Portland with local musi-cians and national acts for 4 days. The **Time-Based Art Festival** (☎ 503/242-1419; www.pica.org/tba) consists of 10 days of modern visual and performance arts spon-sored by the Portland Institute for Contemporary Arts.

Mid- to late October is the sea-son of **harvest festivals**—pumpkin patches, hayrides, corn mazes, and so on—at farms around the city. Many of these happen on Sauvie Island, 10 miles northwest of Port-land on U.S. 30. In mid-November, the **Northwest Film & Video Festi-val** (☎ 503/221-1156; www.nwfilm.org/festivals) brings a host of short films, documentaries, and features by independent filmmakers from the Pacific Northwest.

WINTER   Get in the holiday mood with the **Festival of Lights at the Grotto** (☎ 503/254-7371; www.thegrotto.org). For the entire month of December, this Catholic sanctuary on NE Sandy Boulevard is lit by 500,000 lights, with puppet shows, a petting zoo, choral performances, and plenty of hot chocolate. Speak-ing of lights, mid-December brings the **Christmas Ships Parade** to the

Columbia and Willamette rivers, with upwards of 50 ships decked out in holiday lights after dark. Head to the Oregon Zoo for the **ZooLights Festival** (www.oregonzoo.org), which includes music, kids' activities, and a special holiday train.

The **Portland International Film Festival** (☎ 503/228-7433; www.nwfilm.org) in February brings 100 films from all over the world to theaters around the city. This same month, the Oregon Convention Center becomes one huge bistro during the **Oregon Seafood and Wine Festival** (www.pdxseafood andwinefestival.com), which happily coincides with the Dungeness crab season.

The Weather

Ah yes, the weather. If this almost suspiciously appealing city has a catch, it's what goes on outside from about October to May: mostly gray skies and mist or light rain, with infrequent downpours and sunny days. Hotel rates are lower and reservations are easier to score from fall through spring, particularly along the coast. Bring rain gear and a jacket or fleece for night. (Strangely, nothing brands you as a tourist like using an umbrella.) Temperatures regularly drop into the low 40s in the heart of winter, when the Cascades are being buried in snow.

But, as locals are quick to remind you, the summers are wonderful, even if they don't reliably start, weather-wise, until the 5th of July. Then you can usually count on 3 months of near-constant sunshine with hardly a drop of precipitation for weeks on end. (Portlanders joke that their lawns are brown in the summer and green in the winter.) Temperatures seldom climb above the low 90s, although summer temps have spiked into the low-100s and stayed there for 3 or 4 days in recent years. This is when

hotel and car reservations become essential, especially on the weekends and *especially* on the coast.

Spring and fall are more of a gamble, with occasional windows of sunny weather lasting for a few days or even a few weeks. Even then it's a good idea to have an extra layer ready, ideally one that's waterproof.

Useful Websites

- **www.oregonian.com** is the website for the daily *Oregonian* newspaper.

- **www.wweek.com** takes you to the *Willamette Week* weekly newspaper site.

- **www.portlandmercury.com** is the website of the *Portland Mercury*, another popular weekly.

- **www.travelportland.com** is for the Portland Visitor's Association.

- **www.pdxpipeline.com** offers music, art, and entertainment listings.

- **www.pdxkidscalendar.com** is the place to go for children's events and activities.

- **www.opentable.com**: This popular reservation site offers information about and reservations for PDX eateries.

Car Rentals

All major car-rental companies have desks at the airport, which is the most convenient place to pick up a car. Across from the baggage-claim area you'll find Alamo, Avis, Budget, Dollar, Enterprise, Hertz, National, and Thrifty. Weekly rates for an economy car in summer can run from $200 to $350, with no discounts, so it's a good idea to comparison shop before you book. Rates drop in the rainy months.

PORTLAND'S AVERAGE MONTHLY TEMPERATURE & RAINFALL

	JAN	FEB	MAR	APR	MAY	JUNE
Temp. (°F)	40	43	46	50	57	63
Temp. (°C)	4	6	8	10	14	17
Days of Rain	18	16	17	14	12	10

	JULY	AUG	SEPT	OCT	NOV	DEC
Temp. (°F)	68	67	63	54	46	41
Temp. (°C)	20	19	17	12	8	5
Days of Rain	4	5	8	13	18	19

If you're visiting from abroad and plan to rent a car in the U.S., keep in mind that foreign driver's licenses are usually recognized in the U.S., but you may want to consider obtaining an international driver's license.

Getting There

By Plane
Portland International Airport
(PDX; ☎ 877/739-4636 or 503/460-4234; www.flypdx.com), located 10 miles northeast of downtown along the Columbia River, is an astonishingly pleasant and efficient airport. You can get maps and brochures from the information booth by the baggage-claim area. Some hotels have courtesy shuttle service to and from the airport, especially the ones nearby; be sure to ask when you make a reservation. Carriers flying to PDX include:

- **Air Canada** (☎ 888/247-2262; www.aircanada.ca)

- **Alaska Airlines** (☎ 800/252-7522; www.alaskaair.com)

- **American Airlines** (☎ 800/433-7300; www.aa.com)

- **Condor Air** ☎ 866-960-7915; www.condorair.com)

- **Delta** (☎ 800/221-1212; www.delta.com)

- **Frontier** (☎ 800/432-1359; www.flyfrontier.com)

- **Hawaiian Air** (☎ 800-367-5320; www.hawaiianair.com)

- **Horizon Air** (☎ 800/547-9308; www.horizonair.com)

- **JetBlue** (☎ 800/538-2583; www.jetblue.com)

- **Seaport Air** (☎ 888-573-2767; www.seaportair.com)

- **Southwest** (☎ 800/435-9792; www.southwest.com)

- **Spirit Air** (☎ 800/772-7117; www.spirit.com)

- **United** (☎ 800/864-8331; www.united.com)

- **Virgin America** (☎ 877/359-8474; www.virginamerica.com)

To get downtown by car, follow the signs to downtown via I-205 and I-84 west, and then cross the Willamette River using the Morrison Bridge exit. Without traffic, the trip can take 15 minutes.

Taxis wait outside baggage claim; a ride downtown costs between $40 and $45. **Blue Star** ☎ 503/249-1837; www.bluestarbus.com) runs a shared shuttle bus to the airport for $14 per person each way to and from downtown.

You can also get into the city from the airport by **MAX light-rail.** Trains leave the airport station on the lower level daily about every 15 minutes between 5am and midnight. It takes 35 to 40 minutes to get to Pioneer Courthouse Square in the heart of downtown. To reach destinations in the southeast, northeast, and northwest parts of the city, you can get off at an earlier stop and transfer to a city bus, streetcar, or another MAX line. The adult MAX fare is $2.50 (seniors, or "Honored Citizens," ride for $1.25). For further public transport information, see Getting Around, below.

By Car

Portland is 175 miles south of Seattle; 285 miles south of Vancouver, British Columbia; 640 miles north of San Francisco; and 1,015 miles north of Los Angeles, all via **I-5,** the interstate backbone of the West Coast. Starting in Portland, **I-84** runs east to Idaho and Utah.

By Train

Amtrak trains stop at the historic **Union Station,** 800 NW 6th Ave. (☎ 800/872-7245 or 503/273-4860; www.amtrak.com), 12 blocks from Pioneer Courthouse Square. *The Coast Starlight* train from Seattle to Los Angeles stops at Portland, as well as Sacramento, San Francisco, and Santa Barbara. *The Empire Builder* heads east to Chicago via

Spokane, St. Paul/Minneapolis, and Milwaukee. The sleek, European-style **Amtrak *Cascades*** (www.amtrak cascades.com) train makes the run between Portland and Seattle in 3½ hours (versus 4½ hours for the regular train). The whole Cascades route extends from Eugene, Oregon, to Vancouver, British Columbia. On either type of train, one-way fares between Seattle and Portland run from about $40 to $110, depending on the season.

Taxis are usually waiting outside Union Station. The MAX light-rail green and yellow lines stop about a block away at NW 6th Avenue, and Hoyt Street, and bus routes 7, 9, and 33 stop within a block of the station to the south, toward downtown.

By Bus

The **Greyhound Bus Lines** station is at 550 NW 6th Ave. (☎ 800/231-2222 or 503/243-2361; www.greyhound.com), just across NW Irving Street from Union Station. The Union Station/NW 6th & Hoyt Street MAX stop (green and yellow lines) is right outside, as are stops for city bus routes 7, 9, and 33.

Bolt Bus (☎ 877/265-8287; www.boltbus.com) is a super-cheap bus service between Portland, Eugene, Seattle, and Vancouver, BC. Prices between Seattle and Portland range from about $14 to $25 depending on demand. It departs and arrives at SW Salmon Street between 5th and 6th avenues.

Getting **Around**

Portland encourages the use of public transportation, and you can easily travel around the city via bus, MAX light rail, or the Portland Streetcar, all operated by **TriMet**

(☎ 503/238-7433; www.trimet.org). The TriMet website is useful for planning trips. Note that the Portland Streetcar has a separate website: www.portlandstreetcar.org.

Navigation

Portland addresses are always tagged with a map quadrant: **NE** (northeast), **SE** (southeast), **SW** (southwest), **NW** (northwest) and **N** (north). The dividing lines are the Willamette River between east and west and Burnside Street between north and south. (Burnside itself is split into "East" and "West" on either side of the river.) All of downtown is SW (southwest). You may find the same street name on both sides of the river, just in different quadrants—say, SW Salmon Street and SE Salmon Street. The only exception is North Portland, a big wedge of the city on the east side of the Willamette between I-5 (to the east) and the river (to the west). Addresses here are simply "North" whatever.

Other navigational quirks: Avenues run north to south and streets run east to west; street names in Northwest Portland are alphabetical heading north from Burnside to Wilson; and on the west side, what would be 7th and 8th avenues are instead named Broadway and Park avenues, respectively.

By Light Rail

Portland's light-rail system, the **Metropolitan Area Express** (MAX), connects downtown with the airport, the eastern suburb of Gresham, the western suburbs of Beaverton and Hillsboro, North Portland, and Milwaukie to the south. Train service begins at 5am and runs until midnight. Note that MAX cars have hooks for hanging bicycles inside.

By Streetcar

The **Portland Streetcar** (www.portlandstreetcar.org) runs a 4-mile NS (north-south) route from the South Waterfront District through downtown and the Pearl District to NW 23rd and Marshall. The A and B Loops run clockwise and counterclockwise along a circular 3½-mile route, crossing the river via the Broadway Bridge and the new Tilikum Crossing bridge (opened in 2015). This route connects downtown with the Moda Center, the Convention Center, the Lloyd District, and OMSI. Streetcars run about every 13 to 20 minutes daily from 5:30am to 11:30pm on weekdays, 7:15am to 11:30pm on Saturday, and 7:15am to 10:30pm on Sunday.

By Bus

TriMet buses operate daily over an extensive network, stretching from Forest Grove to Gresham and from North Portland to Oregon City. Just over half the bus lines run about every 15 minutes during the morning and afternoon rush hours on weekdays. Service is less frequent in the early morning, midday, and evening. Buses run from about 5am to 1 or 2am, depending on the route. Every bus has a rack on the front that can hold two bikes. You can find out when the next bus is arriving at your stop by calling **TriMet** at ☎ 503/238-7433 and entering the ID number posted on the bus stop.

Fares

Fares are the same for MAX and buses: $2.50 for adults, $1.25 for seniors 65 years and older, and $1.50 ages 7 through 17. Streetcar fares are slightly lower: $2 for adults, $1.25 for seniors and youth. A ticket is valid for 2 hours. You can also buy an all-day ticket for $5, which is valid on buses, streetcars, and MAX. Buy tickets or day passes at vending machines at bus, light rail, and streetcar stops, in vending machines on board the streetcar, or at the TriMet Ticket Office, 701 SW Sixth Ave., in Pioneer Courthouse Square (open Mon–Fri

8:30am–5:30pm, Sat 10am–4pm). You can also buy tickets at most local Albertsons, Fred Meyer, and Safeway stores. If you buy a ticket on the bus, you'll need exact change.

By Car

Oregon drivers tend to be on the civil side; if you honk your horn in anything but a serious situation, you'll get funny looks (or worse). And don't even try to pump your own gas: Oregon and New Jersey are the only two states where attendants are required to do this for you. It's illegal to text or talk on a cellphone while driving without using a hands-free accessory—and even that's illegal if you're under 18.

You may turn right on a red light after a full stop, and if you are in the far-left lane of a one-way street, you may turn left into the adjacent left lane of a one-way street at a red light after a full stop. Everyone in a moving vehicle is required to wear a seat belt. Drivers must always stop for pedestrians in striped pedestrian crossings.

Portlanders are generally used to driving with bicyclists on the road, but visiting drivers should be extra wary, especially at night and in the rain, because some bikers refuse to use lights or wear helmets. As traffic goes, Portland ranks in the top 20% of cities with bad congestion nationwide. I-5, I-84, and I-205 all often back up during rush hour, when bridges and interchanges turn into chokepoints. Ironically, as more and more people move to Portland because of its "livability," the traffic problem has gotten a lot worse. The I-5 corridor between Portland and Vancouver, Washington, qualifies as a real traffic nightmare and should be avoided between 8 and 10am and 3 and 7pm.

Many of the blocks in downtown, the Pearl District, and the Lloyd District have electronic SmartMeter pay stations for **street parking.** These take cash and credit cards and spit out parking receipts that you attach to your curbside window. One benefit is that you can use your remaining time at another parking space. You're generally required to pay from 8am to 7pm Monday through Saturday and 1 to 7pm on Sunday, and the rate is $1 to $2 per hour.

The best parking deal in town is the six city-owned **SmartPark garages** (☎ 503/790-9300) downtown with nearly 4,000 public spaces. Four of these are open 24/7. Rates are $1.60 per hour for the first hour and $3 to $5 per hour after that. All-day parking is $12 to $15. You'll find SmartPark garages at 1st Avenue and Jefferson Street, 4th Avenue and Yamhill Street, 10th Avenue and Yamhill Street, 3rd Avenue and Alder Street, O'Bryant Square, Naito Parkway and Davis Street, and Station Place (in the Pearl District near Union Station). Hundreds of downtown merchants validate SmartPark tickets for a short stay if you spend a certain minimum, although this varies.

A car is by far the best way to access points outside the city. There just isn't any other way to get to the more remote natural spectacles or to fully appreciate such regions as the Oregon coast or the Columbia River Gorge.

It takes about 2 hours to drive from Portland to Cannon Beach on the Oregon coast; from Portland to Mount Hood, about 1½ hours, depending on traffic.

Car-sharing in America was born in Portland in 1998, and today **Zipcar** has hundreds of vehicles parked around the metro area. They have an office downtown at 739 SW 10th Ave. and Yamhill Street (☎ 503/328-3539 or 866-494-7227; www.zipcar.com).

The **American Automobile Association** (www.aaa.com) has a Portland office at 600 SW Market St. (☎ 503/222-6767 or 800/452-1643), which offers free city maps to members.

By Taxi

Although there are almost always taxis waiting in line at major hotels, you won't find them cruising the streets—you'll have to call ahead for one. **Broadway Cab** (☎ 503/227-1234; www.broadwaycab.com) charges $2.50 per mile and $1 for each additional passenger, with a $2.50 airport pickup surcharge.

Uber (www.uber.com) ride service is also available in Portland.

By Bike

Have you gathered by now that Portlanders are somewhat fond of **bicycling**? Being chosen as the country's first platinum-level Bicycle Friendly Community from the League of American Bicyclists in 2009 is just one of the city's many cycling accolades. A progressive citywide bike transportation program includes ubiquitous bike racks and wide, clear bike lanes on most major commuter routes. Riders are required to obey all traffic laws—cops give out real tickets for not coming to a full stop at stop signs, for instance—and you have to give pedestrians right-of-way on sidewalks (obviously). For more information and news about biking in Portland, check out **BikePortland** (www.bikeportland.org) or the nonprofit **Bicycle Transportation Alliance** (☎ 503/226-0676; www.bta4bikes.org).

Cross a bike with a taxi and you get a **pedicab.** You can hail these three-wheeled cycles-for-hire downtown or call ahead for a pickup. Rates vary—most short trips are $10–$20—and drivers work for tips. Try **PDX Pedicabs** (☎ 503/828-9888; www.pdxpedicab.com) or **Portland Pedicabs** (☎ 503/329-2575; www.portlandpedals.com). Both offer special guided tours of local brewpubs, distilleries, and the like.

Fast **Facts**

AREA CODE   The area code for most of Portland is **503**, with **971** as the new additional code. For the rest of Oregon, the area codes are **541** and **458**.

BABYSITTERS   If your hotel doesn't offer babysitting services, call **Northwest Nannies** (☎ 503/245-5288; www.nwnanny.com).

BUSINESS HOURS   In general, stores are open weekdays 9 or 10am to 5 or 6pm, and Sunday noon to 5pm. Malls can stay open to 9pm Monday to Saturday, while many art galleries and antiques stores close on Monday. Banks are open Monday to Friday 9am to 5pm (occasionally Sat 9am–noon). Bars and clubs can stay open until 2am.

DENTIST   Contact the **Multnomah Dental Society** (☎ 503/513-5010; www.multnomahdental.org) for a referral.

DISABLED TRAVELERS   Wheelchair users will find most of the city relatively flat, outside of the West Hills and Mount Tabor. Buses, MAX light-rail, and the Portland Streetcar are all equipped with lifts for wheelchairs. Most hotels provide wheelchair-accessible rooms, and some of the larger and more expensive

The Savvy Traveler

hotels also have TDD telephones and other amenities for the hearing- and sight-impaired. Sidewalk ramps are the norm downtown but are more randomly placed elsewhere. Organizations that offer resources and assistance to travelers with disabilities include the **American Foundation for the Blind** (☎ 800/232-5463; www.afb. org); and the **Society for Accessible Travel & Hospitality** (☎ 212/447-7284; www.sath.org).

DOCTORS   See "Hospitals," below.

DRINKING LAWS   The legal minimum drinking age in Oregon is 21. Beer and wine are available in grocery stores and convenience stores, and hard liquor can be purchased in bars, restaurants, and liquor stores. Brewpubs tend to sell only beer and wine, but some also have hard liquor licenses.

ELECTRICITY   The U.S. uses 110–120 volts AC (60 cycles). You'll need a 110-volt transformer and a plug adapter with two flat parallel pins to use 220–240 volt appliances. (It's best to bring one from home.)

EMBASSIES & CONSULATES   All embassies are in the U.S. capital, Washington, D.C. There are also consulates in some major U.S. cities, though none are in Portland. Most nations also have a mission to the United Nations in New York City. If your country isn't listed below, call for directory information in Washington, D.C. (☎ 202/555-1212) or check www.embassy.org/embassies.

The embassy of **Australia** is at 1601 Massachusetts Ave. NW, Washington, D.C. 20036 (☎ 202/797-3000; www.usa.embassy.gov. au). Consulates are in New York, Honolulu, Houston, Los Angeles, and San Francisco.

The embassy of **Canada** is at 501 Pennsylvania Ave. NW, Washington, D.C. 20001

(☎ 202/682-1740; www.can-am. gc.ca/washington). Canadian consulates are in Buffalo (New York), Detroit, Los Angeles, New York, and Seattle.

The embassy of **Ireland** is at 2234 Massachusetts Ave. NW, Washington, D.C. 20008 (☎ 202/462-3939; www.embassyofireland. org). Irish consulates are in Boston, Chicago, New York, San Francisco, and other cities. See website for complete listing.

The embassy of **New Zealand** is at 37 Observatory Circle NW, Washington, D.C. 20008 (☎ 202/328-4800; www.nzembassy.com). New Zealand consulates are in Los Angeles, Salt Lake City, San Francisco, and Seattle.

The embassy of the **United Kingdom** is at 3100 Massachusetts Ave. NW, Washington, D.C. 20008 (☎ 202/588-6500; http://ukinusa. fco.gov.uk). Other British consulates are in Atlanta, Boston, Chicago, Cleveland, Houston, Los Angeles, New York, San Francisco, and Seattle.

EMERGENCIES   Dial **911** for fire, police, and medical emergencies.

HOLIDAYS   Government offices, post offices, banks, and many restaurants, stores, and museums are closed on the following national holidays: January 1 (New Year's Day), the third Monday in January (Martin Luther King, Jr. Day), the third Monday in February (Presidents' Day), the last Monday in May (Memorial Day), July 4 (Independence Day), the first Monday in September (Labor Day), the second Monday in October (Columbus Day), November 11 (Veterans Day), the fourth Thursday in November (Thanksgiving Day), and December 25 (Christmas). Banks and offices may also be closed on Election Day, which (in election years) is the

Tuesday after the first Monday in November.

HOSPITALS Hospitals convenient to downtown include **Oregon Health & Science University,** 3181 SW Sam Jackson Park Rd. (☎ 503/494-8311; www.ohsu.edu), **Providence Portland Medical Center,** 4805 NE Glisan St. (☎ 503/574-6595; http://oregon.providence.org), and **Legacy Good Samaritan,** 1015 NW 22nd Ave. (☎ 503/413-7711; www.legacyhealth.org). Legacy has a physician referral service at ☎ 503/335-3500.

INSURANCE For information on traveler's insurance, trip cancelation insurance, and medical insurance while traveling, please visit www.frommers.com/planning.

INTERNET & WI-FI Most of Portland's coffee shops offer free Wi-Fi, as do the branches of the **Multnomah County Library** (☎ 503/988-5402; www.multcolib.org), which also have Internet terminals available to all. Most hotels offer free Internet access as well.

LEGAL AID While driving, if you are pulled over for a minor infraction (such as speeding), never attempt to pay the fine directly to a police officer; this could be construed as attempted bribery, a much more serious crime. Pay fines by mail, or directly into the hands of the clerk of the court. If accused of a more serious offense, say and do nothing before consulting a lawyer. In the U.S., the burden is on the state to prove a person's guilt beyond a reasonable doubt, and everyone has the right to remain silent, whether he or she is suspected of a crime or actually arrested. Once arrested, a person can make one telephone call to a party of his or her choice. The international visitor should call his or her embassy or consulate.

LGBT TRAVELERS Though it has seen more than its share of anti-gay rights battles, Portland has always been a fairly tolerant city. Same-sex couples have been able to marry in Oregon since 2014. To find out what's going on in the LGBT community, pick up a free copy of the bimonthly *Just Out* (☎ 503/236-1252; www.justout.com). The **Gay & Lesbian Community Yellow Pages** (☎ 503/230-7701; www.pdxgayyellowpages.com) lists gay-owned and gay-friendly businesses. Also check with Portland's **LGBT Q Center** (www.pdxqcenter.org).

MAIL The main post office in Portland is at 715 NW Hoyt St. (☎ 800/ASK-USPS or 503/525-5398; www.usps.com). It's open Monday through Friday from 8am to 6:30pm, Saturday from 8:30am to 5pm.

NEWSPAPERS & MAGAZINES The *Oregonian* is Portland's major daily newspaper, followed by the biweekly *Portland Tribune*. The *Portland Mercury* and *Willamette Week* are free arts-and-entertainment weeklies.

PASSPORTS Virtually every air traveler entering the U.S. is required to show a passport.

For Residents of Australia: Call Australian Passport Information Service (☎ 131-232, or visit www.passports.gov.au).

For Residents of Canada: Passport Office, Department of Foreign Affairs and International Trade, Ottawa, ON K1A 0G3 (☎ 800/567-6868; www.ppt.gc.ca).

For Residents of Ireland: Passport Office, Setanta Centre, Molesworth St., Dublin 2 (☎ 01/671-1633; www.foreignaffairs.gov.ie).

For Residents of New Zealand: Passports Office, Department of Internal Affairs, 47 Boulcott St., Wellington, 6011 (☎ 0800/225-050 in New Zealand or 04/474-8100; www.passports.govt.nz).

For **Residents of the United Kingdom:** Visit your nearest passport office, major post office, or travel agency or contact the Identity and Passport Service (IPS), 89 Eccleston Square, London, SW1V 1PN (☎ 0300/222-0000; www.ips.gov.uk).

PHARMACIES Conveniently located downtown pharmacies include **Rite Aid,** 622 SW Alder St. (☎ 503/226-6791), which is open weekdays 7am to 11pm, and **Central Drug,** 538 SW 4th Ave. (☎ 503/226-2222). Fred Meyer and Safeway grocery stores have pharmacies as well.

POLICE The **Portland Police Bureau**'s central precinct is at 1111 SW 2nd Ave. (☎ 503/823-0000; www.portlandpolice.com). Dial **911** for emergencies.

SAFETY Portland is a relatively safe city, but you should take some precautions if you're visiting the Chinatown and Old Town districts at night. Don't leave anything valuable in your car while you're hiking in Forest Park. As a general rule, avoid deserted areas, especially at night, and don't go into public parks at night. Park in well-lit, busy areas whenever possible.

SMOKING Smoking is banned in public indoor spaces throughout the state of Oregon, even bars, as well as within 10 feet of entrances, exits, and windows.

TAXES Oregon is one of only five states with no sales tax, making it a shopper's delight. In Portland, there are 12.5% taxes on both hotel rooms and car rentals (plus an additional fee of 10%–15% if you pick up your rental car at the airport).

TIME Portland is on Pacific time, 3 hours behind Eastern Standard Time, and 8 hours behind Greenwich Mean Time. In the summer, daylight saving time is observed and clocks are set forward 1 hour.

TIPPING Waiters generally receive 15%–20% of the bill; taxi drivers 15% of fare; bartenders $1 per drink; hotel chamber staff $1–$2 per day; skycaps and valets $1–$2 per bag; and valet parking attendants $1 per ride.

TOILETS Portland may be the only city with its own patented public toilet, the **Portland Loo** (www.portlandloo.com). Find these sleek, solar-powered, 24-hour restrooms along SW Naito Parkway in Waterfront Park at both SW Ash and SW Taylor streets, as well as at NW Glisan Street between SW 5th and 6th avenues, and at Jamison Square at NW Johnson Street and NW 11th Avenue. Otherwise, look for restrooms in most Starbucks and hotel lobbies.

VISAS The U.S. State Department has a **Visa Waiver Program (VWP)** allowing citizens of the following countries to enter the United States without a visa for stays of up to 90 days: Andorra, Australia, Austria, Belgium, Brunei, Czech Republic, Denmark, Estonia, Finland, France, Germany, Greece, Hungary, Iceland, Ireland, Italy, Japan, Latvia, Liechtenstein, Lithuania, Luxembourg, Malta, Monaco, the Netherlands, New Zealand, Norway, Portugal, San Marino, Singapore, Slovakia, Slovenia, South Korea, Spain, Sweden, Switzerland, and the United Kingdom. (**Note:** This list was accurate at press time; for the most up-to-date list of countries in the VWP, consult www.dhs.gov/visa-waiver-program.) Even though a visa isn't necessary for citizens of those countries, in an effort to help U.S. officials check travelers against terror watch lists before they arrive at U.S. borders, visitors from VWP countries must register online through the **Electronic System for Travel Authorization (ESTA)** before boarding a plane or a boat

Cannabis Laws

In 2015, Oregon voters approved the sale and possession of recreational marijuana in small amounts to adults 21 and older. A number of new "pot boutiques" are licensed by the state and strictly controlled, requiring proof of age before you are allowed to enter. You may not legally smoke pot on the street or in any public space.

to the U.S. Travelers must complete an electronic application providing basic personal and travel eligibility information. The Department of Homeland Security recommends filling out the form at least 3 days before traveling. Authorizations will be valid for up to 2 years or until the traveler's passport expires, whichever comes first. Currently, there is a US$14 fee for the online application. For more information, go to www.dhs.gov/visa-waiver-program. **Canadian citizens** may enter the United States without visas, but will need to show passports and proof of residence.

Citizens of all other countries must have (1) a valid passport that expires at least 6 months later than the scheduled end of their visit to the U.S.; and (2) a tourist visa.

Portland: **A Brief History**

15,000–13,000 B.C. Cataclysmic floods carve the Columbia Gorge, with waters reaching as high as Crown Point.

12,300 B.C. Earliest known human inhabitants in Oregon, near Paisley, 220 miles southeast of Eugene.

1579 English explorer Sir Francis Drake reaches the mouth of the Rogue River in southwest Oregon, turned back by "thicke and stinking fogges."

1792 American captain Robert Gray becomes first to sail into the Columbia River, names it in honor of his ship the *Columbia Rediviva*.

1805 Expedition led by Meriwether Lewis and William Clark reaches the Pacific Ocean at the mouth of the Columbia River, and spends a miserable winter in Fort Clatsop.

1819 Spain cedes all lands above 42 degrees north latitude (California's northern boundary today) to the U.S.

1824 Fort Vancouver, fur-trading outpost of the Hudson's Bay Company, founded across the Columbia River from present-day Portland.

1841 Bartleson-Bidwell Party, the first group to make a wagon crossing of the Oregon Trail, reaches the Willamette Valley from Missouri.

1843 Business partners Asa Lovejoy and William Overton pay 25¢ filing fee to claim 640 acres on the west bank of the Willamette River in present-day Portland; settlers elect provisional government.

1844 Oregon City becomes first incorporated town west of the Rocky Mountains.

1845 Asa Lovejoy and new partner Francis Pettygrove flip a coin to name the settlement called simply "The Clearing"; Pettygrove wins and names it after his hometown of Portland, Maine.

1840s–1860s About 400,000 emigrants travel west on the Oregon Trail.

1848 Oregon becomes first U.S. territory west of the Rockies; Pettygrove sells nearly the entire townsite of Portland to tanner Daniel Lownsdale for $5,000 worth of leather, despite only owning half of it.

1851 City of Portland incorporated.

1879 First telephone lines installed.

1880 First electric street lights arrive.

1883 Northern Pacific Railroad reaches Portland.

1889 Local newspapers call Portland "the most filthy city in the Northern States" with sidewalks that would be a "disgrace to a Russian village."

1905 Lewis and Clark Centennial Exposition held, including the Forestry Building, "the world's greatest log cabin."

1907 Oaks Amusement Park opens; first Rose Festival held.

1908 Portland Police Department hires Lola Greene Baldwin, the nation's first policewoman.

1915 Columbia River Gorge scenic highway constructed.

1940s Portland's Kaiser shipyards become the world's leading shipbuilders due to the war effort. Portland becomes a boomtown as tens of thousands of workers, including the first African-Americans, flock to Portland for war-related work.

1946 Portland State University founded.

1948 A dike holding back the Columbia River collapses and floodwaters destroy the hastily constructed public housing community known as Vanport, built in north Portland for war-industry workers; 15 are killed.

LATE 1940s–1950s Organized crime, corruption, and vice dominate local politics, resulting in indictments of the Multnomah county district attorney and Portland's mayor and chief of police. In 1949, Dorothy McCullough Lee is elected the first female mayor of Portland and promises to rid the city of gambling, corruption, and prostitution.

1957 Elvis Presley performs in front of 14,000 people at Multnomah Stadium (now Providence Park), one of the first outdoor stadium rock concerts.

1960s Winemakers plant Oregon's first pinot noir vines in the Umpqua Valley, southwest of Eugene, starting modern era of Oregon winemaking.

1964 Nike founded by University of Oregon track runner Philip Knight and coach Bill Bowerman.

1965 The Beatles play two shows at Memorial Coliseum for 20,000 fans, inspiring Allen Ginsberg's poem "Portland Coliseum."

1977 Portland Trail Blazers win NBA Championship for the first and only time (so far).

1980s–1990s Portland is roiled by several costly and virulent anti-gay rights battles.

Portland Reads

Portland has long been a magnet for writers and the readers who love them. There's a long list of books by local authors, about Portland, or both. Here are a few classics:

- Swan Adamson, *My Three Husbands* and *Memoirs Are Made of This*
- Jean M. Auel, *The Clan of the Cave Bear*
- Beverly Cleary, *Ramona the Pest*
- Katherine Dunn, *Geek Love*
- Stewart Holbrook, *The Portland Story*
- Ursula K. Le Guin, *The Lathe of Heaven*
- Donald Olson, *The Pacific Northwest Garden Tour*
- Chuck Palahniuk, *Fugitives and Refugees: A Walk in Portland, Oregon*
- Joe Sacco, *Palestine*

1980 Mt. St. Helens erupts, killing 57 people and blanketing Portland in ash.

1985 First light rail train route opens; *Portlandia* statue installed.

1990s Dot-com boom brings an influx of artists, graphic designers, and Internet entrepreneurs to Portland; dot-com bust brings even more from Seattle and San Francisco.

1993 Vera Katz is elected 49th mayor of Portland and serves until 2005; she is widely considered to be one of Portland's most effective mayors.

1998 Oregon becomes the first state to legalize euthanasia with the Death with Dignity Act.

2000s "Jail Blazers" era of the NBA team is marked by fights and charges of sexual assault, drug possession, and dog fighting.

2001 Portland becomes first city in the U.S. to (re-)introduce modern streetcar service.

2004 Multnomah County starts issuing marriage license to same-sex couples. Over 3,000 gay couples rush to get married.

2005 After a court challenge and public referendum, Multnomah County rescinds same-sex marriage and invalidates all same-sex marriages.

2008 Oregon Legislature passes the Family Fairness Act, allowing same-sex couple to establish domestic partnerships.

2010 *Portlandia* comedy series premieres on IFC, poking fun at the city "where young people go to retire."

2014 Oregon becomes the 15th state to strike down discriminatory marriage laws, making it legal for same-sex couples to wed.

2015 Oregon legalizes growing and possession of small amounts of marijuana for recreational use; pot boutiques open in Portland.

Index

See also Accommodations and Restaurant indexes, below.

Photo **Credits**

PDX Soap Box Derby; p 39: © With Kind Permission Portland Art Gallery; p 40: © Lincoln Barbour Photography/Ground Kontrol; p 41: © James Crawford / Dreamstime.com; p 42: © With Kind Permission Oaks Amusement Park; p 43: © Rigucci / Shutterstock.com; p 45: © KennStilger47 / Shutterstock; p 46: © www.travelportland.com; p 47: © Dtfoxfoto / Dreamstime.com; p 49: © Gino Rigucci / Dreamstime.com; p 51, top: © Jpldesigns / Dreamstime.com; p 51, bottom: © Valentin Armianu / Dreamstime.com; p 52: © Atmosphere1 / Dreamstime.com; p 53: © Jpldesigns / Dreamstime.com; p 55: © Jamie Francis / www.travelportland.com; p 57: © With Kind Permission Clear Creek Distillery; p 59: © With Kind Permission Community Cycling Center; p 60: © Kathleen Nyberg / McMennamin's; p 63: © With Kind Permission Noun; p 64: © With Kind Permission Imelda's Shoes; p 65, top: © Kathleen Nyberg/McMennamin's; p 65, bottom: © With Kind Permisison Portland Parks & Recreation, Portland, OR; p 67: © Jamie Francis/www.travelportland.com; p 68: © With Kind Permission OMSI; p 71, top: © With Kind Permission Oaks Amusement Park; p 71, bottom: © www.travelportland.com; p 73: © With Kind Permission Crafty Wonderland; p 78: © With Kind Permission Crafty Wonderland; p 79: © With Kind Permissions Powell's; p 80: © With Kind Permission Noun; p 81: © With Kind Permission Imelda's Shoes; p 82: © Torsten Kjellstrand / www.travelportland.com; p 83, top: © With Kind Permission Clear Creek Distillery; p 83, bottom: © With Kind Permission Millennium Music; p 84: © With Kind Permission PSU; p 85: © www.travelportland.com; p 87: © Portland Parks & Recreation; p 89: © With Kind Permission Hoyt Arboretum; p 90: © With Kind Permisison Oregon Zoo; p 91: © www.travelportland.com; p 94: © www.travelportland.com; p 95: © Le Pigeon / Carly Diaz; p 96: © With Kind Permission Ava Genes; p 100: © Andina / Lincoln Barbour; p 101: © John Valls / Bar Avignon; p 104: © With Kind Permission Fire on the Mountain; p 105: © Le Pigeon/Carly Diaz; p 106: © With Kind Permission Muselet; p 107: © With Kind Permission Prasad; p 108: © With Kind Permission Ringside Steak House; p 109: © Toro Bravo/John Gorham; p 110: © Erica Schroeder / Dreamstime.com; p 111: © With Kind Permission Driftwood; p 114: © With Kind Permission Bailey's Tap Room; p 116: © With Kind Permission Driftwood; p 117: © Hopworks Brewbar/ Tim LaBarge; p 119: © With Kind Permission Lola's Room; p 120: © Ground Kontrol/Lincoln Barbour Photography; p 121: © Portland Opera/Cory Weaver; p 125: © With Kind Permission Oregon Symphony; p 127: © Max Pucciariello; p 128: © Keller Auditorium/David Barss; p 129: © With Kind Permission Doug Fir Lounge; p 130: © With Kind Permission Timbers; p 131: © Courtesy of The Benson; p 134: © Torsten Kjellstrand / www.travelportland.com; p 136: © With Kind Permission Hotel Lucia; p 138: © With Kind Permission Portland Mayor's Mansion; p 139: © Jess Kraft/ Shutterstock; p 141: © tusharkoley / Shutterstock.; p 143: © Rigucci / Shutterstock.com; p 144: © kan_khampanya / Shutterstock.com; p 145: © Rigucci / Shutterstock.com; p 149: © CWK Photography / Adelsheim Vineyard; p 151: © With Kind Permission Allison Inn & Spa; p 153, top: © B Brown/Shutterstock.com; p 153, bottom: © Sue Stokes / Shutterstock.com; p 155: © Gino Rigucci / Dreamstime.com; p 156: © Stephen Chung/Shutterstock.com; p 157: © Yusia / Shutterstock.com; p 158: © Terry W Ryder / Shutterstock.com; p 159: © Jon Bilous / www.shutterstock.com.

Notes

Notes

Notes